HOW TO
LOSE
WEIGHT
WELL

HOW TO
LOSE
WEIGHT
WELL

THE
COMPLETE
DIET PLANS

STACIE STEWART

Photography by Louise Hagger and John Davis

quadrille

Health warnings

▶ You shouldn't be trying to lose weight if you are underweight or you have, or suspect you have, an eating disorder (including anorexia and bulimia). If you have any history of psychiatric illness, you should seek advice from your GP or at least from a dietitian so that you have someone to check up on you.

▶ If you are under 18 years of age, even if you are overweight, you should seek advice from your GP or from a qualified dietitian. The long-term health consequences of dieting badly when you're young are hard to overstate.

▶ If you are pregnant or breastfeeding, you should discuss any plans to lose weight with your doctor.

▶ If you are frail in any way (recovering from major illness or surgery), again, you should consult your GP or a dietitian.

▶ If you are on any medication, check with your GP or pharmacist.

▶ If you are an insulin-dependent or Type-1 diabetic, review any weight-loss plans with your care team.

▶ If you are actively unwell (fever or other symptoms of illness), this is not the right time to start dieting.

▶ Finally, salt. If you cook from fresh, then it's unlikely you'll be having too much salt. If you're concerned about your health, get your blood pressure checked.

CONTENTS

INTRODUCTION

This is the manual I wish I had had access to whenI started my weight-loss regime. It's a real-life working manual for real people, people who are overweight and overwhelmed by the diet industry, written by someone who has been there and done it. This book is a non-jargon, easy-to-follow guide outlining realistically how to eat healthily and lose weight well, for life. You can dip in and out of it for years depending on your situation and goals. It's full of well-balanced, flavoursome recipes that will make you full of happiness not guilt.

Firstly, before you begin, download a calorie tracking app or keep a little food diary to log all your macros. **What's a macro? Well it's a fancy word for the nutrients contained in foods in the largest amounts, namely carbohydrates (sugars, starches, fibre), lipids (fats) and proteins.** Each of these 'macronutrients' provides energy measured as calories – we will go into further detail on these on pages 10–11. Keeping a journal to track your progress can have a very positive effect and holds you accountable for what you've eaten each day.

Secondly, be honest with yourself about your weaknesses. Mine is kids' cereal! Rid your home of these things to give yourself a fighting chance. Out of sight, out of mind! Are you a secret eater? I was. Constantly eating a handful of nuts here and there, or a sugar in my tea a few times a day. It all adds up and it can strongly contribute to you not achieving your goals, which is so demotivating. I will show you through this book that making small changes, my way, can save you hundreds of calories while sacrificing **NONE** of the flavour.

Thirdly, relocate to an isolated country manor, abandon all belongings and loved ones because this is going to take complete isolation... I'm kidding, that's exactly what this book isn't. This is a book that will fit into yours, mine and anyone's lifestyle.

And last but not least, **BELIEVE** you can do this, set high-stake goals, think what you want to achieve with this book – something that really matters to you. I remember when I saw the preview of *Food Glorious Food* my high-stake goal was to be happier with how I looked before it went on TV. Every time I thought I couldn't do it or wanted to give up, I imagined everyone whispering about how

> BELIEVE you can do this, set high-stake goals, think what you really want to achieve with this book, something that really matters to you.

overweight I was when the show aired a few weeks later. That was my first goal, and I lost around a stone in a month. After that I set a new goal; I think it was to be able to do one unassisted press up (I can now do about 100 without breaking a sweat). It's important with this point to be realistic though; I knew I wasn't going down to go from a size 18 to a 6 in a month!

And here's something to reassure you: there's no denying yourself with this book, no spending £100 on organic exotic fruit or fancy powders to make a cake. This is a simple, accessible guide for *your* lifestyle that works, and I've proved it. It's a life plan for different scenarios and timescales, encompassing the best of all three series of *How to Lose Weight Well*.

I WANT THIS BOOK TO:

▶ **Help you develop a better relationship with food**

▶ **Transform your body for life**

▶ **Help you believe you can make lasting changes to your health and lifestyle like I have**

▶ **Be a manual you refer to time and time again for any situation**

So, we all have a story – what's mine? I was in a position thousands of people in this country are also in: I was overweight and unhealthy and I didn't have a clue what to do about it. I ran a bakery and had a history of poor eating habits. The diet and fitness industry and information online, though vast, were so confusing. Are carbs the enemy? How much protein do I need? What does 'calorie deficit' mean? What kind of cardio should I be doing and for how long? These questions tormented me and at the age of 31 I felt lost and suffocated in an industry I had never even dipped my toe into. Up to that point, dieting to me meant denying myself all day, running up and down my mam's stairs twice, and then eating a French stick. I had no idea about refined carbs, bad sugars – nothing! The final straw came after an appearance on TV when I was criticized for my weight. I cried, and probably ate a few pasties. Then I thought to myself: you can sit and cry and feed your sorrows, or you can prove them wrong. That was 2012.

On 2 January 2013, I started a boot camp at 6.30A.M. with a local personal trainer called Steven Shaw. It was a killer – a massive wake-up call. I was by a mile the biggest in the class and the most unfit. I couldn't even complete the circuit and was deeply embarrassed but I didn't let it show. Through

> This is my transformation plan and it features all the tips and tricks I've picked up along the way. This is how I transformed my body, lifestyle and mind – and you can, too.

sweat and tears (the blood was to come), I turned up three times a week. It was hell. I made excuses not to go – "It's too hot outside", "it's too cold", "my legs are sore" – but at the end of the day I knew I needed to put up and shut up to make a change. I persisted and slowly the fat melted away. I lost a whopping 14lb in the first month and I thought, "wow, I can do this". That little glimmer of hope was all I needed to ignite the spark. The more I lost, the more it motivated me, so I started working more on my diet, watching what I ate and calorie counting. Pretty soon my body and mind were beginning to change. What I quickly discovered was that no matter which diet you're on, **losing weight simply comes down to calories in versus calories out;** the bigger the deficit, the bigger the weight loss in a shorter space of time.

This book aims to set out three different weight-loss plans based on three time periods, all with a different calorie deficit. Of course, all your favourite diets and recipes from the TV show will be appearing throughout the book. A lot of the diets on the show had their own specific health benefits, such as the DASH diet, and some of the diets

on the show, such as carbohydrate-restricting diets, can turbocharge fat loss for some people, so we will be harnessing the power of these, too.

I opened my café Eat Naked in Brighton in 2015. I have maintained my body weight since then, changing my life and career. Now I want you to have the chance to change your life, too. This is my transformation plan; it's exactly how I lost weight, improved my health, significantly reduced my body fat and completely transformed my body, lifestyle and mind.

This is my norm now, the new normal, but you don't have to wait years to achieve what I've achieved. I've put all the knowledge and know-how, tips and tricks I've learned over the last few years into this book. These recipes, and ultimately these meal plans, mean that you can lose weight well for life! I firmly believe that if the recipes are good for you and **FULL OF FLAVOUR**, you're more likely to stick to a diet and find a new way of eating and **ENJOYING** food. My promise is that every choice in this book is a good choice with exciting and simple meal preparation.

MACROS

WE MENTIONED MACROS EARLIER BUT WHAT ARE THEY AND WHY ARE THEY SO IMPORTANT?

PROTEIN is an important building block for bones, muscles, cartilage, skin and blood. Your body uses protein to grow, build and repair tissues, make enzymes, hormones and other body chemicals. Throughout this book I have recommended you include a good protein source with each of your meals as it helps you feel full, therefore helping you to eat less overall. My favourite protein sources are eggs, meat, fish and dairy (Greek yogurt and cottage cheese), but protein is also abundant in nuts and seeds, other grains and pulses and lentils.

CARBOHYDRATES are all about energy. Your body converts carbohydrates to glucose, which is your body's main energy source. Glucose is a type of sugar that can be used straightaway for energy or stored away as glycogen to be used later. The problem is that it's easy to overconsume carbs so once we

have used what we need and stored enough to 'use later', any extra (unneeded) will be converted to fat (but this is true no matter what the source of calories). Unless you have a very physical job or hit the gym for a heavy session most days, I promise that you don't need large portions.

I incorporate different amounts of carbs in my diet depending on my goals and if I've trained that day. However, not all carbs were created equally. There are 'good' carbs, such as whole grains, vegetables, fruits and beans, which are absorbed slowly into our systems, avoiding spikes in blood sugar levels. At the other end of the scale, we have refined and highly processed ('bad') carbohydrates. These are devoid of beneficial fibre and include white bread, biscuits, cakes and confectionery (sweets and chocolate), fizzy drinks, syrups, honey, etc. My favourite carbohydrate sources are brown basmati rice, wholemeal pasta, sweet potatoes, oats, vegetables, pulses (beans and lentils) or quinoa.

FATS are necessary to give your body energy, to provide essential fatty acids, which the body cannot make, and to support cell growth. They also help protect your organs. Fats assist your body in absorbing some nutrients like vitamins and are a part of important hormones. And if all that wasn't enough to make you ditch the 'low-fat' treats for good essential fatty acids, they also support brain performance and memory.

There are three main types of fats, and I've listed some good sources after each one:

▶ Unsaturated: include a few portions a day into your diet – olive oil, walnuts (unsalted), avocados, flaxseeds and oily fish (eat at least once a week but follow the NHS guidelines for the recommended amounts, especially if pregnant or breastfeeding)

▶ Saturated: eat in moderation – meat (choose lean), full-fat dairy

▶ Trans fats: avoid at all costs – manufactured cakes, biscuits, takeaways, pies, pastry (you get the picture!)

I would like to include a quick note on oils. There is so much information in the public domain that it can be confusing and often contradictory, so here's my definitive list.

OIL GUIDE

Thought you knew which oil to drizzle over your salad and which to roast your potatoes with? Think again.

EXTRA VIRGIN OLIVE OIL
▶ Best for: dressing salads, drizzling over pasta. Think of it as a finisher.

OLIVE OIL
▶ Best for: light frying such as falafel, etc. and baking.

RAPESEED OIL
▶ Best for: roasting potatoes, frying.

COCONUT OIL
▶ Best for: occasional use when flavour is required, e.g. in Asian dishes.

If a bottle is labelled 'vegetable oil', check what the oil is, as it can be rapeseed, and make sure it is high in monounsaturated fat.

▸ MY TOP TIPS ◂

1 **DO NOT GIVE UP**. It takes 21 days to form a new habit. If you can do it for 21 days, you can do it for life. There's a reason that you are the way you are, it's easy and convenient and it reflects your lifestyle/work/family commitments. You're going to have to break old habits and form new ones. The first 21 days will be tough as you're out of your routine. I'll say it again: **DO NOT GIVE UP**. Change starts with baby steps. Do you think I ever dreamed all those years ago when I was a size 18 that I would be a size 8, writing a book to help you? Having completely transformed my life? No! How did I achieve it? **BABY STEPS**. Give it your all for 21 days… you can do it!

2 **DON'T WASTE TIME TRYING TO FIND THE PERFECT DIET**. No two people are the same, so why should we all stick to the same diet, calculating points, having different coloured days, and cutting out entire food groups? It's not sustainable for everyone and that's why I follow the 'mostly good enough' diet from this book that covers all the important stuff about weight loss and a healthy lifestyle, but is also a diet which you're able to stick to over time, consistently and realistically.

3 **MASTER PORTION CONTROL**. The visual opposite really helps me consider portion control – just adding a 'little bit more' of a few things can contribute to up to 50 per cent more calories on your plate, even with healthy food.

4 **BELIEVE IN YOURSELF**. Learn to love the journey and you will find yourself on the right path for long-term success.

5 **UNDERSTAND THE LIFECYCLE OF AN EXTREME DIETER**. "I'm unhappy about how I look – I need to make a change – I'm going all in, strict diet, cutting out everything all at once – yes it's working so well I can do this – I've worked so hard, I deserve a treat – oh no, I've messed up, I shouldn't have eaten that – ah well, I've failed I might as well quit"… which leads back to the first point.

6 **CUT YOURSELF SOME SLACK**. Work hard, be patient, **add the good stuff and eventually it will crowd out the bad stuff**, and remember that you're never more than one bite away from being back on track. Consistency will always beat intensity.

► Fat 26.4g; protein 42.4g; carbs 19g; fibre 12.8g; calories 509

► Fat 48.4g; protein 65.8g; carbs 30.4g; fibre 21.2g; calories 862

7 WATCH OUT FOR SNEAKY CALORIES RUINING YOUR GOALS. Licks, bites, nibbles, a few nuts here and there – we are all guilty of it. Every time I make a smoothie at Eat Naked, I help myself to a spoonful of peanut butter. One day I added it all to my calorie-counting app and it was a whopping 400 calories. Plus there are unaccounted-for calories in cooking oils (1 tbsp olive oil = 120 calories) and salad dressings (100g ranch dressing = 400 calories). These things can all add up to hundreds of unplanned calories each day.

8 EAT IT – DELETE IT. Here are a few handy food-swapping tips:

Eat avocado – delete butter. (A smear of avocado contains 5.3g less fat and 0.7g more fibre than an equivalent amount of butter)

Eat spiralized courgettes, i.e. courgetti – delete pasta. (150g courgetti contains 118 fewer calories and 27.4g less carbs than 100g cooked white spaghetti)

Eat fresh fruit – delete sugary snacks.

Eat a homemade PBJ sandwich made from wholegrain bread, good nut butter (no added sugar or salt), and sliced strawberries – delete the white bread, cheap peanut butter (made with processed palm oil) and sugary jam (this swap will save you about 10.4g carbs and raise the fibre by 3g)

9 BEWARE OF CALORIFIC NUTS. Go online and work out what 100 calories of different nuts amount to. Now remember what that looks like – it's a lot less than people think.

10 CHOOSE SNACKS WISELY. Did you know? Half a small packet of crisps contains about the same amount of calories as three whole cups of popped corn.

11 KNOW WHEN YOU'RE OVEREATING. Measure out 1 level tablespoon of peanut butter and spread it on a piece of toast. Most people don't know how much that actually is and tend to spread a lot – it's so easy to overeat.

12 BEWARE OF LIQUID CALORIES AND ALWAYS FACTOR THEM INTO YOUR PLAN. Did you know that your favourite fruity cider has the same amount of calories as a large burger from a fast-food restaurant? But you wouldn't eat six of those in one night... Be drink aware, choose low-calorie mixers and white spirits, and watch out for the added fruit juices and syrupy ingredients in cocktails.

TIPS FOR SHOPPING WISELY

#1 Do not shop while hungry.

#2 Make a list and have a rough plan for meals so that you don't impulse buy.

#3 Load up on fruit and veggies.

#4 Go lean with your protein – think chicken, turkey, lean steak, cottage cheese, 3%-fat Greek yogurt.

#5 Focus on filling 'good' carb sources rather than the 'bad' carb ones we mentioned earlier.

#6 Grab some healthy fats – yes, that includes peanut butter, but just make sure it doesn't contain added sugars, salt or processed palm oil.

#7 Be strategic with your treats – remember what I said about ridding your home of trigger foods? Choose foods which satisfy your cravings but which you can control. It doesn't matter if a packet of four chocolate bars is on offer for the same price as just one bar; just get the one, because if there are four in the house, you'll eat them eventually.

TIPS FOR EATING OUT

#1 Before eating out, adjust earlier meals to allow for a calorie buffer. I go light on breakfast and lunch to allow me to eat what I like later (within reason) while still sticking to my calorie goals.

#2 Figure out what you want to eat before you go. Check menus online and decide on a meal to save you over-ordering 'because you can't think' or because 'the waiter is rushing you' when you're at the restaurant.

#3 Focus on your goal; the people you're with; the atmosphere; the conversation. If you do this you'll be less likely to overeat.

MEAL PLANS

MEAL PLANS

Now that you've read the introduction and tips, it's time to get down to business, put it all into practice and shift some of those stubborn pounds. We all learned on *How to Lose Weight Well* how much everyone loves a plan, especially me. Even now when I'm at a steady, happy body weight, I still have a plan and follow specific macros. When I set out to write this book I wanted to allow a lot of flexibility for everyone's lifestyle but then I thought 'no!' If this was me five years ago, I would WANT to be told what to do. I've taken the best of both worlds with the meal plans, recommending meals but including guidelines if you fancy something different and don't want to get off track. It's the best of both worlds – a plan with flexibility.

The meal plans in the following pages cross-refer to the recipes in this book and are divided into three parts detailing how to lose weight well according to your situation.

#1 KICKSTART How to lose up to 8lb in 12 days.
#2 SHAPESHIFTERS How to lose up to a stone over 6 weeks.
#3 LIFE CHANGERS How to change your approach to eating to achieve long-lasting change.

WEIGHT LOSS IS SIMPLE!

If the amount of calories you eat is more than the calories you burn, you'll gain weight. If the amount of calories you eat is less than the amount of calories you burn, you'll lose weight. If the amount of calories you eat equals the amount of calories you burn, you'll stay the same weight.

There are a number of factors that you need to take into consideration to determine how many calories you'll need to eat to lose weight, as there is no one single number that will work for everyone. It's possible, however, to come up with an estimate for how many calories you need to maintain your weight, which you then adjust to figure out how many calories you should eat to lose weight.

Your BMR is your Basal Metabolic Rate – this is the number of calories your body needs in order to function, day to day.

▶ **To calculate your BMR, take your body weight in lbs. and multiply it by 13.**

Your BMR is a calculation of your ideal daily calorie intake and it's specifically based on your own weight.

Once you have calculated this number, you might find that it seems high, but it's important to trust this number. If you've been struggling to lose weight, it's likely you've been consuming too FEW calories and your body has kicked into starvation mode, which could mean holding on to fat for dear life and breaking down muscle to provide calories (energy). Trust the process and start working on consuming enough calories to match your BMR.

If you have been consuming significantly fewer calories than your BMR then you're going to need to do a little adjusting before you begin any of the meal plans, but it'll be worth it in the long run. Before you begin the Kickstart or Shapeshifters meal plans, you'll need to have your daily calorie intake as close to your BMR as possible for at least a week, ideally two. This may seem counter-productive, but I've been there and, believe me, the pounds dropped in those two weeks of increasing calories as if my body was crying out in joy and 'releasing' from its starvation mode for being properly fed.

Now that you know your daily calorie goal to aim for to lose weight well, how do you get those calories? We briefly mentioned 'calories in' versus 'calories out' earlier. In theory, you can eat whatever you want to achieve those calories – yes, 1,500 calories a day from chocolate and crisps and you'll lose weight – but if you're chomping through high-calorie, low-nutritional-value foods, you'll struggle to hit your macros within your calorie allowance and you'll feel rubbish, too.

▶ Below left: my body on 1,300 calories per day
▶ Below right: 90 days later, on 2,500 calories per day

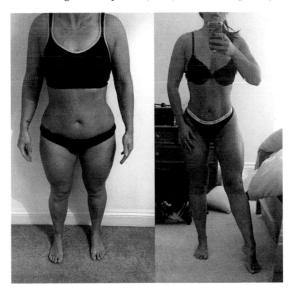

It's **quality** versus **quantity**. Imagine a bowl of Greek yogurt, fruit and healthy granola versus a chocolate bar: both have the same calorific value but it comes down to nutritional value – how are they going to make you feel? The yogurt is a natural, high-protein source with no chemicals or added sugar, the nutty granola contains healthy fats and there's added fibre and vitamins from the fruits. All in all it's a pretty nutrient-packed, nourishing snack to help you feel fuller and more satisfied for longer. Conversely the chocolate is full of sugar, refined (bad) carbohydrates, saturated (bad) fats and is heavily processed with significant 'empty' calories providing energy but little in the way of nourishment. I'm not here to tell you which one to choose; if you want the chocolate bar, go for it. But if you truly want to change your lifestyle, you will have to change your thinking and make better choices 80 per cent of the time.

▶ Right and far right: both of these foods contain roughly the same calorie count, but one has far more nutrients and will keep you fuller for much longer

A POINT ON WEIGHING YOURSELF

I never weigh myself any more. For me, it's how I feel in my clothes that counts. I do measure myself occasionally and have my body fat checked at my local gym. When I began my journey, my body fat was 46%; it's now around the 18–24% mark. If you would like to weigh yourself, always weigh yourself at the same time each week, preferably first thing in the morning after you have been to the toilet and before you have eaten or drunk anything. Your first fluids in the morning should be hot water with a squeeze of lemon juice, or a lemon and ginger herbal tea. Drink 1.5–2 litres of water per day, no matter what plan you are on.

MEAL PLAN
KICKSTART

This is a 12-day plan – three fasting days and nine non-fasting days. Once you have your BMR, we are going to work to a 500-calorie deficit for each non-fasting day, and a total of 500 calories on each fasting day, in order to lose up to 8lb in 12 days. To turbo-charge this, I recommend burning 300 calories minimum on four of those non-fasting days through exercise.

My exercise is metabolic conditioning or HIIT training, as they are quick and effective (a 20-minute HIIT session can burn 300 calories or more). I also love to do a quick fitness DVD at home before work. Think of joining a gym as most offer these types of classes for free and training in a group really pushes you. Be active in your daily life, too, not just through exercise. E.g., walk rather than taking the car, use the stairs, get up from your desk regularly, park a bit further away from your destination or get off the bus a stop early and walk the rest of the way. It all adds up!

Once you have completed the plan, your body may adjust and weight loss will slow down. **Do not** drop your calories again – this is a kickstart diet and is not meant for long-term weight loss. It's a one-off diet for fast results. Switch to the Shapeshifters plan now.

For our Kickstart plan, we are going to keep our carb intake low. Carb-restricting diets have proved very successful on *How to Lose*

Weight Well with one contributor shedding a whopping 5 stone in 4 months. Your objective is to kickstart your weight loss by helping your body switch to burning fat and quickly eliminate any 'bad' carb or sugar cravings you may have – because if you maintain a daily balance of fat, protein and fibre, you avoid the blood-sugar drops that lead to cravings.

'Fasting' does not mean that you eat nothing at all. For the Kickstart plan you will be eating 500 calories (for women) and 600 calories (for men). I've recommended this be done in two meals but if three small, high-volume, low-calorie meals suit you, there's plenty to choose from in this book. Just use the macros key and choose high-protein meals with lots of veggies which tend to fill you up more.

Because you are only fasting for three days out of 12, you won't feel like you are depriving yourself for long. This helped me on my path to losing 5 stone, as it was easy to stick to.

Over the next 12 days we will be eliminating almost all carb-containing foods such as grains, legumes, certain fruits, juices, sugars, honey, sweets, desserts and starchy veg. The target is to eat no more than 35g carbs per day which is the average needed to get your body into a ketogenic state – the state in which some of the body's energy supply comes from ketone bodies in the blood (i.e. using up the body's fat stores) rather than from blood glucose. Most of these carbs will come from high-fibre veg with additional fibre sourced from nuts and seeds. We won't be skimping on healthy fats; along with protein and fibre, fat is crucial to keep you full between meals.

We are all different shapes and sizes, and therefore will all yield a different BMR. To keep things simple and allow flexibility in this book, I've worked out meal plans for 1,300 calories per day.

▶ **So, if you weigh 150lbs, your BMR = 1,950 calories (150 x 13). On this Kickstart plan, because we are aiming for a 500-calorie deficit, your daily target would be 1,450 calories (1,950 - 500). Since my meal plans here total 1,300 calories per day, this would allow you the freedom to mop up those leftover 150 calories each day with whatever you like. When you are mopping up, just remember to keep your carbs to a minimum and not to exceed 35g; I have added the remaining net carbs to the start of each day of the meal plan. (You don't need to monitor your other macros when you're mopping up – just your calories and carbs.)**

If you are making your own choices, you'll need to know how to work out the **net carbs**. Simply remove the fibre from the total carbs on the macros key, as fibrous carbs are 'free carbs' and don't have to be included in your daily totals. E.g., if a dish has 15g carbs but 6 of them are fibre, the net carbs = 9g.

Feel free to add your own spices and seasonings to all recipes – chilli, salt, pepper, lemon, even herbs – as they are low-calorie 'free foods' and can add extra flavour.

If you choose to make swaps through the meal plans, that's fine, but log what you're eating and **be honest**. Using an app such as MyFitnessPal calculates all this for you and makes life so easy. I really recommend it, or at the very least, keep a little food diary.

So, here goes... Good luck!

MONDAY

(This will leave 5g net carbs to consume.) If you would like to weigh yourself, do so this morning using the tips on page 24.
Breakfast: 1 serving of Paleo Granola (page 44) with 1 small pot of organic natural yogurt.
Lunch: 1 serving of Asian Raw Slaw & Ginger Salad with Toasted Cashews (page 63) with 100g chicken breast.
Dinner: 2 x Spelt & Spinach Crêpes with Loads of Toppings (page 66) filled with ½ avocado (mashed) and 75g smoked salmon, split between the 2 crêpes. Serve with a rocket side salad (no dressing).

TUESDAY

(This will leave 5g net carbs to consume.)

Breakfast: My Ultimate Post-Workout Shake (page 148) without the frozen banana.

Lunch: 1 serving of Salmon with Cheat's Creamy Cucumber & Dill Salad (page 76).

Dinner: 1 serving of Herby Low-Carb Meatballs in Marinara (page 82), with 1 spiralized courgette.

▶ TIP FOR DESSERT ◀

▶ 2 scoops (100ml) of OPPO salted caramel ice cream.

▶ GET AHEAD ◀

Whizz up half a batch of the Green Goddess Dip (i.e. 3 servings) (page 51).

WEDNESDAY (FIRST FAST DAY)

Only water, coffee, green and herbal teas before midday, and do not eat after 6P.M. Use your judgement on the coffee – I'm not talking about a grande latte with whipped cream from your local coffee shop! Choose semi-skimmed milk, nut milks or black coffee only.

Ladies: follow the plan as below.

Gents: feel free to add 100 calories of walnuts (approximately 12 nuts) OR feta cheese (approximately 40g) OR add the peanut butter to My Go-To Classic Green Smoothie as per the recipe.

▶ **Meal 1** – My Go-To Classic Green Smoothie without the peanut butter (page 49).

▶ **Meal 2** – Amazing Volumetric Turkey Salad without the walnuts and cheese (page 62).

▶ GET AHEAD ◀

Make the Protein Muffin Frittatas (page 160), keep 4 muffins (2 servings) out and freeze the rest.

THURSDAY

(This will leave 12g net carbs to consume.)

Breakfast: 1 serving of Protein Muffin Frittatas (page 160) with 1 serving of Green Goddess Dip (page 51).

Lunch: 1 serving of Sesame Chicken Salad with Cucumber Noodles & Sweet Chilli Dipping Sauce (page 116).

Dinner: 1 serving of Crunchy Punchy Vietnamese Beef Salad (page 78) and 1 serving of Avocado Cacao Mousse (page 172).

▶ GET AHEAD ◀

Marinate the chicken for tomorrow's Reinvented Tandoori Chicken BBQ (page 86).

FRIDAY

(This will leave 8g net carbs to consume.)

Breakfast: 1 serving of Paleo Granola (page 44) with 1 small pot of organic natural yogurt.

Lunch: 1 serving of Protein Muffin Frittatas (page 160) with 1 serving of Green Goddess Dip (page 51) and a large, leafy green salad, and 1 x Raw Tahini Goji Bite (page 152).

Dinner: 1 serving of Reinvented Tandoori Chicken BBQ (page 86).

SATURDAY

(This will leave 20g net carbs to consume.)

Breakfast: Sneaky Popeye Omelette with any topping ideas (page 46).

While you're pottering in the kitchen, make a batch of Almond Butter Cups (page 186).

Lunch: My Go-To Classic Green Smoothie, (page 49) and 1 x Almond Butter Cup (page 186).

Dinner: 1 serving of Baked cod with a Pine Nut Crust & Spinach Mornay (page 91) with your final portion of Green Goddess Dip (page 51).

SUNDAY

(This will leave 5g net carbs to consume.)

Breakfast: 1 serving of Low-Carb Cream Cheese Pancakes (page 45).

▶ **TIP** ◀

▶ Use your extra calories for topping the pancakes. I like Greek yogurt and berries.

Lunch: 1 serving of Throw-It-In Beef Rendang (page 132) without the mango chutney (freeze the other serving).

▶ **TIP** ◀

▶ Use your extra calories for cauliflower rice (page 139) or steamed green veg.

Dinner: 1 serving of Cashew Chicken with Courgetti & Coriander (page 136) without the sweet chilli dipping sauce.

MONDAY (SECOND FAST DAY)

Only water, coffee, green and herbal teas before midday, and do not eat after 6P.M. Gents: add half a frozen banana to My Ultimate Post-Workout Shake (page 148), and for My Pad Thai with Peanut Sauce (page 96), up your chicken to 150g for your additional 100 calories.

▶ **Meal 1** – My Ultimate Post-Workout Shake (page 148) without the frozen banana.

▶ **Meal 2** – 1 serving of My Pad Thai with Peanut Sauce (page 96) with 100g chicken breast shredded through (make 2 servings and store one for tomorrow).

TUESDAY

(This will leave 10g net carbs to consume.)

Breakfast: My Ultimate Post-Workout Shake (page 148) without the frozen banana, and 1 x Raw Tahini Goji Bite (page 152).

Lunch: 1 serving of My Pad Thai with Peanut Sauce (page 96) with 100g chicken breast shredded through.

Dinner: 1 serving of Turkey Mince Lettuce Cups with Spicy Avocado Dip & Tomato Salsa (page 80).

▶ GET AHEAD ◀

Take 2 Protein Muffin Frittatas and the Throw-It-In Beef Rendang out of the freezer.

WEDNESDAY

(This will leave 10g net carbs to consume.)

Breakfast: 1 serving of Protein Muffin Frittatas (page 160).

Lunch: 1 serving of Throw-It-In Beef Rendang (page 132).

▶ TIP ◀

▶ Use your extra calories for sides.

Dinner: 1 serving of Turkey Feta Burgers with Corn & Chilli Lime Butter (page 108).

▶ GET AHEAD ◀

Take 1 Protein Muffin Frittata out of the freezer.

THURSDAY (THIRD FAST DAY)

Only water, coffee, green and herbal teas before midday, and do not eat after 6P.M. Gents: try adding 1 tbsp good-quality extra virgin oil to your Low-Carb Italian Chilli Crab 'Pasta' (page 144) for the extra 100 calories, or have 2 Protein Muffin Frittatas.

▶ **Meal 1** – 1 serving of Low-Carb Italian Chilli Crab 'Pasta' (page 144) with 50g salad leaves (no dressing).

▶ **Meal 2** – 1 x Protein Muffin Frittata (page 160) and 1 x 2-Minute Naughty Pot (page 171).

FRIDAY (THE FINAL DAY)

(This will leave 9g net carbs to consume.)

Breakfast: 1 serving of Smoked Salmon & Cannellini Bean Dip (page 162) with 1 medium carrot cut into batons, 1 celery stick cut into batons and 1 pepper of choice cut into strips.

Lunch: 1 serving of Moroccan Sesame Carrot Salad (page 74).

Dinner: 1 serving of Thai Poached Salmon Bowl (page 112) and 1 x Almond Butter Cup (page 186).

SATURDAY (WEIGH-IN DAY)

Weigh yourself, if you like, using the tips on page 24.

MEAL PLAN SHAPESHIFTERS

Once you have your BMR, we are going to work to a 400-calorie deficit to lose 2lb per week, healthily. To turbo-charge this, I recommend burning 300 calories, three days a week, through exercise. My favourites are metabolic conditioning or HIIT training as they are quick and effective (a 20-minute HIIT session can burn 300 calories or more). I also love to do a quick fitness DVD at home before work. Think of joining a gym as most offer these types of classes for free and training in a group really pushes you. Be active in your daily life, too, not just through exercise. E.g., walk rather than taking the car, use the stairs, get up from your desk regularly, park a bit further away from your destination or get off the bus a stop early and walk the rest of the way. It all adds up!

Once you have completed 6 weeks on this plan, your body may adjust and weight loss will slow. **Do not** drop your calories again – this is a Shapeshifters diet and is not meant for long-term weight loss. Simply switch to the Transformers plan at this point.

We are all different shapes and sizes, and therefore will all yield a different BMR. To keep things simple and allow flexibility I've worked out meal plans for 1,300 calories (see sample calculation on page 27). This will allow freedom to mop up those extra calories with whatever you like.

The overleaf is a sample two-week meal plan. As the Shapeshifters is a six-week plan, for your final four weeks you can either repeat the given plan, or, if you have the confidence, you can make your own choices.

Feel free to add your own spices and seasonings to all recipes – chilli, salt, pepper, lemon, even herbs – as they are low-calorie 'free foods' and can add extra flavour.

If you choose to make swaps through the meal plans, that's fine, but log what you're eating and **be honest**. Using an app such as MyFitnessPal calculates all this for you and makes life so easy. I really recommend it, or at the very least, keep a little food diary.

WEEK 1

MONDAY

If you would like to weigh yourself, do so this morning using the tips on page 24.

Breakfast: 1 serving of Banana Bread (page 168).

▶ TIPS ◀

▶ Use your extra calories for yogurt and berries, or peanut butter.

▶ Portion the banana bread into 12, keep one more slice out and freeze the remaining 10 slices individually.

Lunch: 1 serving of Asian Raw Slaw with Toasted Cashews (page 63) with 100g chicken breast.

Dinner: 1 serving of Prawn, Courgette & Quinoa Patties (3 patties) (page 122) on a bed of lettuce of choice, with 1 serving of Spicy Avocado Dip (page 80).

▶ TIPS ◀

▶ Make 2 servings of the Prawn, Courgette & Quinoa Patties and keep one for tomorrow.

▶ Make both servings of the Spicy Avocado Dip (i.e. the whole recipe) and keep one for tomorrow.

TUESDAY

Breakfast: My Ultimate Post-Workout Shake (page 148).

Lunch: The leftover Prawn, Courgette & Quinoa Patties (3 patties) (page 122) from dinner last night, with a large, leafy green salad and the final serving of Spicy Avocado Dip (page 80).

Dinner: 1 serving of Herby Low-Carb Meatballs in Marinara (page 82) with 1 courgette, spiralized or julienned.

▶ GET AHEAD ◀

Make the Turmeric All-Day Granola Bars (page 48).

WEDNESDAY

Breakfast: 1 serving of Banana Bread (page 168).

▶ TIP ◀

▶ Use your extra calories for yogurt and berries, or peanut butter.

Lunch: 1 serving of Salmon with Cheat's Creamy Cucumber & Dill salad (page 76) on a bed of lettuce of choice, and 1 serving of Turmeric All-Day Granola Bars (page 48).

Dinner: 1 serving of One-pot Black Lentil Chilli with Spicy Cauliflower Rice (page 139).

► Make both portions of One-pot Black Lentil Chilli with Spicy Cauliflower Rice and keep one for tomorrow.

THURSDAY

Breakfast: 1 serving of Turmeric All-Day Granola Bars (page 48).
Lunch: 1 serving of One-pot Black Lentil Chilli with Spicy Cauliflower Rice (page 139).
Dinner: 1 serving of Crunchy-Punchy Vietnamese Beef Salad (page 78) and 1 x Avocado Cacao Mousse (page 172).

► TIP ◄
► Make 2 x Avocado Cacao Mousses and chill one for another day.

► GET AHEAD ◄
Marinate the chicken for tomorrow's Reinvented Tandoori Chicken BBQ (page 86) and make a batch of Paleo Granola (page 44).

FRIDAY

Breakfast: 1 serving of Paleo Granola (page 44) with 1 small grated apple and 1 small pot of organic natural yogurt all mixed together for a quick, tasty bircher.
Lunch: 1 serving of Flash Prawns in a Jar with Crunchy Salad & Nam Jim (page 118).
Dinner: 1 serving of Reinvented Tandoori Chicken BBQ (page 86).

SATURDAY

Breakfast: 1 serving of High-Carb Banana Protein Pancakes (3 pancakes) (page 45).

► TIP ◄
► Use your extra calories for extra toppings, but I love Greek yogurt, berries and honey.

Lunch: 2 x Spelt & Spinach Crêpes with Loads of Toppings (page 66) filled with ½ avocado (mashed) and 75g smoked salmon, split between the 2 crêpes. Serve with a rocket side salad (no dressing).
Dinner: Sesame Chicken Salad with Cucumber Noodles & Sweet Chilli Dipping Sauce (page 116) and 1 x Avocado Cacao Mousse (page 172).

SUNDAY

Breakfast: 1 x Sneaky Popeye Omelette with any topping idea (page 46).
Lunch: My Go-To Classic Green Smoothie (page 49).
Dinner: 1 serving of Throw-It-In Beef Rendang (page 132) without the Mango Chutney (freeze the other serving).

► TIP ◄
► Use your extra calories to allow for the mango chutney or any additional sides such as rice, or spicy cauliflower rice (page 139).

Make the Protein Muffin Frittatas (page 160), the Green Goddess Dip (page 80) and the Almond Butter Cups (page 186).

WEEK 2

MONDAY

Breakfast: 2 x Protein Muffin Frittatas (page 160) with 1 serving of Green Goddess Dip (page 80).

Lunch: 1 serving of My Pad Thai with Peanut Sauce (page 96) with 100g chicken breast shredded through.

Dinner: 1 serving of Courgette Fritters (2 fritters) (page 50) with a poached egg and a large, green leafy salad and 1 serving of Green Goddess Dip (page 80), and 2 x Almond Butter Cups (page 186).

► GET AHEAD ◄

Make the Raw Vegan Tahini Goji Bites (page 152).

TUESDAY

Breakfast: My Ultimate Post-Workout Shake (page 148) and 2 x Raw Vegan Tahini Goji Bites (page 152).

Lunch: 1 serving of Moroccan Sesame Carrot Salad (page 74) with 100g chicken breast.

Dinner: 1 serving of Turkey Mince Lettuce Cups with Spicy Avocado Dip & Tomato Salsa (page 80).

► TIP ◄

► Make full portions of both the Spicy Avocado Dip and Tomato Salsa (page 80) and keep the other portions for tomorrow.

WEDNESDAY

Breakfast: 2 x Protein Muffin Frittatas (page 160) and 2 x Raw Vegan Tahini Goji Bites (page 152).

Lunch: 1 serving of Smoked Salmon & Cannellini Bean Dip (page 162) with 1 medium carrot cut into batons, 1 celery stick cut into batons and 1 pepper of choice cut into strips.

Dinner: 1 serving of Turkey Feta Burgers with Corn & Chilli Lime Butter (page 108) without the corn and chilli lime butter. Serve the patties wrapped in iceberg with the Avocado Dip and Tomato Salsa (page 80) leftover from last night.

► TIP ◄

► Use your additional calories to treat yourself to the corn and chilli lime butter (page 108).

Take the Throw-It-In Beef Rendang
(page 132) out of the freezer.

THURSDAY
Breakfast: My Ultimate Post-Workout Shake
(page 148).
Lunch: 1 serving of leftover Throw-It-In Beef
Rendang (page 132) reheated until piping hot
throughout. Choose your own sides based on
your calories left for the day.
Dinner: 1 x serving of Jewelled Tabbouleh
with Harissa Roast Aubergine (page 64).

FRIDAY
Breakfast: My Go-To Classic Green
Smoothie (page 49).
Lunch: 2 x Protein Muffin Frittatas (page
160) with a green salad and 1 serving of Spicy
Avocado Dip (page 80).
Dinner: 1 serving of Chicken Tikka Masala
(make both portions and freeze one) (page 92)
with a green salad, and 2 x Almond Butter
Cups (page 186).

SATURDAY
Breakfast: 1 serving of Huevos Rancheros
with Wholemeal Tortilla (page 58).
Lunch: 1 serving of Thai Poached Salmon
Bowl (page 112).

Dinner: 1 serving of Middle Eastern Stuffed
Aubergine with Freekeh Pilaf, without the
freekeh pilaf (page 126).

▶ TIP ◀
▶ To use your extra calories for the day, have
the freekeh pilaf with your Middle Eastern
Stuffed Aubergine.

SUNDAY
Breakfast: 1 serving of Teff pancakes with
Sweet Dukkah & Fruit Compote (2 pancakes)
(page 56).
Lunch: 1 serving of Sweetcorn Fritters
(2 fritters) (page 50) on a bed of rocket with
1 serving of Spicy Avocado Dip & Tomato
Salsa (page 80).
Dinner: 1 serving of Monday's Crispy Lamb
with Lemony Three-Bean Smash & Lots of
Herbs (page 84).

▶ TIP ◀
▶ To use your extra calories for the day, have
a side, or a cheeky small glass of wine.

MEAL PLAN
TRANSFORMERS

Once you have your BMR, in order to maintain a healthy lifestyle – changing your eating habits and losing a few pounds on the way – you simply have to work to your BMR. You have the pick of the recipes in this book, and complete flexibility within your new lifestyle as long as you're logging your food and hitting your calorie targets. This Transformers plan isn't about quick fixes that will help shift a few stubborn pounds; it's about health, happiness, confidence and transforming your body and mindset for life. Believe me: it's possible and I've done it.

As this is a long-term plan, I would aim for the 80/20 approach – that is, 80 per cent healthy, well-balanced choices from this book, and 20 per cent allowances for you to indulge and keep your sanity. This is a life plan not a crash diet, after all, and you need flexibility, but as you begin to transform I promise you those '20 per cent' choices will become healthier and healthier. Aim for more carbohydrates on those days when you hit the gym (after you've trained) to help you repair and recover. This plan is based around three meals a day and includes lean protein in most of your meals. I've included a two-week sample meal plan to get you on track.

We are all different shapes and sizes, and therefore will all yield a different BMR. To keep things simple and allow flexibility I've worked out meal plans for 1,300 calories (see sample calculation on page 27). This will allow freedom to mop up those extra calories with whatever you like.

Feel free to add your own spices and seasonings to all recipes – chilli, salt, pepper, lemon, even herbs – as they are low-calorie 'free foods' and can add extra flavour.

If you choose to make swaps through the meal plans, that's fine, but log what you're eating and **be honest**. Using an app such as MyFitnessPal calculates all this for you and makes life so easy. I really recommend it, or at the very least, keep a little food diary.

WEEK 1

MONDAY
If you would like to weigh yourself, do so this morning using the tips on page 24.
Breakfast: 1 serving of Banana Bread (page 168).

▶ TIPS ◀
▶ Use your extra calories for yogurt and berries, or peanut butter.
▶ Portion the banana bread into 12, keep one more slice out and freeze the remaining 10 slices individually.

Lunch: 1 serving of Moroccan Sesame Carrot Salad with 100g chicken breast (page 74).
Dinner: 1 serving of Prawn, Courgette & Quinoa Patties (3 patties) (page 122) on a bed of lettuce of choice.

▶ TIPS ◀
▶ Make 2 servings of the Prawn, Courgette & Quinoa Patties and keep one for tomorrow.
▶ Make both servings of the Spicy Avocado Dip for tomorrow.

TUESDAY
Breakfast: My Go-To Classic Green Smoothie (page 49).
Lunch: The leftover Prawn, Courgette & Quinoa Patties (3 patties) (page 122) from dinner last night, with a large, leafy green salad and the first serving of Spicy Avocado Dip (page 80).
Dinner: 1 serving of Post-Gym Super Wholefood Nutty Salad (page 104) with 100g chicken breast and the final serving of Spicy Avocado Dip (page 80) from last night.

▶ GET AHEAD ◀
Make the Turmeric All-Day Granola Bars (page 48).

WEDNESDAY
Breakfast: 1 serving of Banana Bread (page 168).

Lunch: 1 serving of Crunchy-Punchy Vietnamese Beef Salad (page 78) with a large handful of lettuce.
Dinner: 1 serving of One-pot Black Lentil Chilli with Spicy Cauliflower Rice (page 139) and 1 serving of Turmeric All-Day Granola Bars (page 48).

▶ TIP ◀
▶ Make both portions of One-pot Black Lentil Chilli with Spicy Cauliflower Rice (page 139) and keep one for tomorrow.

THURSDAY
Breakfast: My Ultimate Post-Workout Shake (page 148).
Lunch: 1 serving of One-pot Black Lentil Chilli with Spicy Cauliflower Rice (page 139).
Dinner: 1 serving of Baked Cod with a Pine Nut Crust & Spinach Mornay (page 91) and 1 x Avocado Cacao Mousse (page 172).

▶ TIP ◀
▶ Make 2 x Avocado Cacao Mousses (page 172) and chill one for another day.

▶ GET AHEAD ◀
Marinate the chicken for tomorrow's Reinvented Tandoori Chicken BBQ (page 86) and make the Paleo Granola (page 44).

FRIDAY

Breakfast: My Ultimate Post-Workout Shake (page 148).
Lunch: 1 serving of Tuna Poke (page 154).
Dinner: 1 serving of Reinvented Tandoori Chicken BBQ (page 86).

▶ TIP ◀

▶ Use your extra calories for rice or bread.

SATURDAY

Breakfast: 1 x Sneaky Popeye Omelette with any topping idea (page 46).
Lunch: My Go-To Classic Green Smoothie (page 49).
Dinner: 1 serving of Throw-It-In Beef Rendang (page 132) (freeze the other portions).

▶ TIP ◀

▶ Use your extra calories for sides, such as rice or spicy cauliflower rice (page 139).

SUNDAY

Breakfast: 1 serving of High-Carb Banana Protein Pancakes (3 pancakes) (page 45).

▶ TIP ◀

▶ Use your extra calories for extra toppings, but I love Greek yogurt, berries and honey.

Lunch: 1 serving of Spelt & Spinach Crêpes with Loads of Toppings (2 crêpes) (page 66) filled with ½ avocado (mashed) and 75g smoked salmon, split between the 2 crêpes. Serve with a rocket side salad (no dressing).
Dinner: 1 serving of Sesame Chicken Salad with Cucumber Noodles & Sweet Chilli Dipping Sauce (page 116) and 1 x Avocado Cacao Mousse (page 172).

▶ GET AHEAD ◀

Make the Protein Muffin Frittatas (page 160), the Green Goddess Dip (page 80) and the Almond Butter Cups (page 186).

WEEK 2

MONDAY

Breakfast: 2 x Protein Muffin Frittatas (page 160) with 1 serving of Green Goddess Dip (page 80).
Lunch: 1 serving of Coconut Mung Bean Daal (page 102) with 100g chicken breast shredded through.

▶ TIP ◀

▶ Freeze the other portion of Coconut Mung Bean Daal (page 102) for another day.

Dinner: 1 serving of Courgette Fritters (2 fritters) (page 50) with a poached egg, a large, green leafy salad and 1 serving of Green Goddess Dip (page 80), and 2 x Almond Butter Cups (see page 186).

▶ GET AHEAD ◀

Make the Raw Vegan Tahini Goji Bites (page 152).

TUESDAY

Breakfast: My Ultimate Post-Workout Shake (page 148) and 2 x Raw Vegan Tahini Goji Bites (page 152).

Lunch: 1 serving of Sesame Kale Salad (page 103) with 100g chicken breast.

Dinner: My Pad Thai with Peanut Sauce (page 96) with 150g prawns.

▶ **GET AHEAD** ◀

Make the Protein Muffin Frittatas (page 160), keep 4 out (2 servings) and freeze the other 8 (4 servings).

WEDNESDAY

Breakfast: 2 x Protein Muffin Frittatas (page 160) and 2 x Raw Vegan Tahini Goji Bites (page 152).

Lunch: 1 serving of Smoked Salmon & Cannellini Bean Dip (page 162) with 1 medium carrot cut into batons, 1 celery stick cut into batons and 1 pepper of choice cut into strips, with the salsa/dip leftover from last night as a dipping platter.

Dinner: 1 serving of Baked Quick Creamy Risotto (page 90).

▶ **GET AHEAD** ◀

Take the Throw-It-In Beef Rendang (page 132) out of the freezer.

THURSDAY

Breakfast: My Ultimate Post-Workout Shake (page 148).

Lunch: 1 serving of leftover Throw-It-In Beef Rendang (page 132) reheated until piping hot. Choose sides based on your available calories.

Dinner: 1 x serving of Jewelled Tabbouleh with Harissa Roast Aubergine (page 64).

FRIDAY

Breakfast: 2 x Protein Muffin Frittatas (page 160) with a green salad and 1 serving of Green Goddess Dip (page 80).

Lunch: My Go-To Classic Green Smoothie (page 49).

Dinner: 1 serving of Chicken Tikka Masala (page 92) (make both portions and freeze one), and 1 serving of Instant Banana Ice Cream (page 182) – choose your flavour.

SATURDAY

Breakfast: 1 serving of Teff pancakes with Sweet Dukkah & Fruit Compote (2 pancakes) (page 56).

Lunch: 1 serving of Sweetcorn Fritters (2 fritters) (page 50) on a bed of rocket and 1 serving of Spicy Avocado Dip (page 80).

Dinner: 1 serving of Sag Gosht, Coriander Salsa & Bombay Sweet Potatoes (page 140).

▶ **TIP** ◀

▶ To use your extra calories for the day, have a side, or a cheeky small glass of wine.

SUNDAY

Breakfast: 1 serving of Huevos Rancheros with Wholemeal Tortilla (page 58).

Lunch: 1 serving of Thai Poached Salmon Bowl (page 112).

Dinner: 1 serving of Middle Eastern Stuffed Aubergine with Freekeh Pilaf, without the freekeh pilaf (page 126).

▶ **TIP** ◀

▶ To use your extra calories for the day, have the freekeh pilaf with your Middle Eastern Stuffed Aubergine.

Using the macros key, feel free to swap and change items on the meal plan to your taste or according to what you are able to do in a day. Some days will be easier than others and you'll have more time to prep and plan; other days you'll be up and out and 300 miles up the country with a takeaway latte before 8A.M. PLAN for these days and factor these things into your food for the day. This is YOUR weight-loss plan, YOUR dreams, YOUR goals... so, eyes on the prize, guys. You can do this!

NUTRITIONAL INFORMATION

All nutritional information is per serving. All eggs are medium. Invest in measuring spoons (mine were from a pound shop); never guesstimate portions.

RECIPES

BREAKFAST
& BRUNCH

I don't want to be one of those people who write a recipe for avocado and poached eggs on toast. I'm sure we can all whack a mashed-up avo on some bread and sprinkle it with chilli, lime and salt. It's a healthy, balanced breakfast and you can pimp it with best-quality thinly sliced tomatoes, bacon or turkey bacon, sautéed greens, and you can even sneak in more healthy fats from seeds, too. Perfect! Nut butters and fruit on toast are another favourite. Try to avoid using packaged bread – choose high-quality homemade breads from local bakers instead, as it will make all the difference. Some of my favourites are sourdough, wholegrain, rye and spelt. Enjoy these recipes from my kitchen to yours.

FAT (g): 23.8
PROTEIN (g): 5.5
CARBS (g): 4.7
FIBRE (g): 3.3
CALORIES: 262
MAKES: 15 PORTIONS

I love granola but the majority of shop-bought brands are loaded with sugar. Here I've added a very small amount of maple syrup. I make this granola in bulk and keep it in an airtight container for up to two weeks. This is my go-to breakfast when my fats are a little higher and I'm keeping the carbs low. My favourite way to serve it is with yogurt and berries; however, I love snacking on this omega-rich granola when I'm on the go, too.

PALEO GRANOLA

100g coconut flakes
100g ground almonds
50g pumpkin seeds or seeds of choice
100g flaked almonds
100g pecans, chopped
100ml melted coconut oil
3 tbsp maple syrup, honey or coconut sugar
  or feel free to leave out all together
1 tsp ground mixed spice or ground cinnamon
1 tsp vanilla extract
pinch of salt

"Trust me: most shop-bought granola is full of sugar. Make your own and you'll have a nutritious breakfast for several days."

Preheat the oven to 160°C/gas mark 3 and line a baking tray with baking paper.

In a very large bowl, combine the coconut flakes, ground almonds, pumpkin seeds, flaked almonds and pecans.

In another bowl, combine the coconut oil, maple syrup, spice, vanilla and salt. Add the wet ingredients to the dry ingredients and stir until the dry ingredients are thoroughly coated. Spread the granola in a thin layer on the prepared baking tray and bake in the oven for 12–15 minutes until golden, stirring halfway through to prevent burning.

The granola will firm up and stick together once it's cooked so you can either break it up or give it a quick pulse in a food processor.

FAT (g): 8.3
PROTEIN (g): 16.9
CARBS (g): 31.6
FIBRE (g): 2
CALORIES: 273
SERVES: 1 (MAKES 3 PANCAKES)

Hitting your protein macros doesn't have to mean chicken breasts and eggs all day. I enjoy these protein pancakes several times a week with different toppings depending on my calorie allowance for the day.

PROTEIN PANCAKES, TWO WAYS

HIGH-CARB BANANA PROTEIN PANCAKES

1 small banana
½ scoop of good-quality whey protein powder
1 tbsp flour of choice
1 egg
pinch of salt
½ tsp vanilla extract (optional)
1 tsp coconut oil or low-cal fry spray, for frying

Mash the banana with a fork in a bowl, then whisk in the remaining ingredients, except the oil. Heat a little coconut oil or fry spray in a pan over a medium-high heat. When hot, add 2 tbsp of the batter per pancake and cook until bubbles appear on the surface, about 2 minutes. Flip over and fry until golden brown and crisp, 1–2 minutes. Serve. I like them with a little honey and a few slices of banana.

FAT (g): 14.8
PROTEIN (g): 29.4
CARBS (g): 4
FIBRE (g): 3.8
CALORIES: 274
SERVES: 1 (MAKES 3–4 PANCAKES)

LOW-CARB CREAM CHEESE PANCAKES

1 egg, separated
1 tbsp good-quality whey protein powder
1 tbsp coconut flour (this is important as it's the lowest carb)
pinch of salt
¼ tsp baking powder
1 tbsp full-fat cream cheese
1 tsp coconut oil or low-cal fry spray, for frying

Beat the egg yolk, protein powder, flour, salt, baking powder and cheese together in a bowl until combined.

In a separate bowl, whisk the egg white until stiff, then gently fold it into the egg yolk mixture. The mix will be thick and as light as a feather.

Heat a little coconut oil or low-cal fry spray in a non-stick frying pan over a medium-high heat. When hot, add 2 tbsp of the batter per pancake and cook until bubbles appear on the surface, about 2 minutes. Flip over and fry the other side until golden brown and crisp, 1–2 minutes. Serve. I like them with Greek yogurt and a few berries.

FAT (g): 14.7
PROTEIN (g): 22.3
CARBS (g): 2.2
FIBRE (g): 2.8
CALORIES: 235
SERVES: 1

High in protein and healthy fats, this omelette is a great start to any day! Top with your favourite veggies as a sneaky way to fill up on your 5-a-day. Make these super-thin and use them as a 'wrap' for a tasty grab-and-go breakfast burrito, and don't forget to serve with a squeeze of lemon, as vitamin C helps your body absorb plant-based iron found in the spinach.

SNEAKY POPEYE OMELETTE

a little low-cal fry spray or ½ tsp butter or coconut oil, for frying
3 eggs
splash of milk
100g spinach
salt and pepper

Preheat a frying pan. I like to use a good non-stick pan, or one spray of low-cal fry spray, but if you have the calorie allowance go for ½ tsp butter or coconut oil. Beat the eggs and milk in a bowl.

Add the spinach to the hot pan and sauté for 1 minute until wilted, then pat the spinach dry on kitchen paper and roughly chop. Leave the pan over a medium heat.

Add the spinach to the beaten eggs and whisk well, then season with salt and pepper.

Add the eggs to the pan and move the pan around to spread the mix out evenly. When the omelette begins to firm up, but is still a little raw on top, you have two options: either fill with one of the delicious topping ideas below and finish under a medium-hot grill for 2–4 minutes until golden and set, or if you want to add your toppings later, using a spatula, ease around the edges of the omelette, then fold it over in half. When it starts to turn golden brown underneath, remove the pan from the heat and slide the omelette onto a plate, then top or fill to your heart's content.

TOPPING IDEAS

Tomato, basil, feta & red onion: Add diced tomatoes, torn basil, 25g crumbled feta and a little finely chopped red onion. You can take the heat out of the onion with a squeeze of lime if you prefer, or sauté it briefly to soften.

Avocado, chilli, coriander & lime: Add ½ medium avocado, chopped into chunks with a good squeeze of lime, fresh or dried chillies and a few tbsp finely chopped coriander.

Chorizo, tomato & smoked paprika: Add 20g chopped chorizo gently sautéed for a few minutes in a frying pan to release its oils, then throw in a medium diced tomato and ½ tsp smoked paprika. This is delicious as a hot or cold filling.

FAT (g): 12.7
PROTEIN (g): 5.1
CARBS (g): 21.1
FIBRE (g): 2.4
CALORIES: 202
MAKES: 10

As I'm up and out for 7A.M. I can't bring myself to eat that early, and by the time I'm in the kitchen at Eat Naked it's non-stop until lunch, so when it gets to 1P.M. I find I've forgotten to eat. For this reason, I've started creating some easy grab-and-go breakfasts. These turmeric granola bars are packed with slow-release carbohydrates, immune-boosting ingredients and healthy fats, which make a perfect breakfast, pre- or post-gym snack or just a simple treat. We sell a tray of these a day in the deli. As with most granola bars, they are easy to adapt and mix up according to whatever you have in your cupboard. Not only that but you can cut them to size for your calorie allowance.

TURMERIC ALL-DAY GRANOLA BARS

"It might seem odd to put pepper in these bars but it's vital to help the body absorb the antioxidants in the turmeric."

50g mixed seeds of choice
50g nuts of choice, roughly chopped
180g jumbo oats
1 tsp ground turmeric
1 tsp vanilla extract
1 medium banana, mashed
50g dried fruits of choice (optional)
pinch of salt and pepper
50g coconut oil
3 tbsp coconut sugar

Preheat the oven to 160°C/gas mark 3. Line an 8 x 8cm tin with baking paper.

Lightly toast the seeds and nuts in a dry frying pan for 3–5 minutes, stirring occasionally, until golden; this develops their flavour. Tip into a bowl and stir in the oats, turmeric, vanilla, banana, dried fruits (if using), salt and pepper.

Melt the coconut oil and sugar together either in a small saucepan or in a microwaveable bowl in the microwave in short bursts. Pour over the oat mixture, stir well and add the dried fruit, if using. Pat the mixture into the prepared tin and bake in the oven for 20–25 minutes until golden and the edges are crisp. The mixture will firm up once cooled so don't be tempted to overcook it.

Once cooled, remove from the tin and cut into 10 small bars.

FAT (g): 16.8
PROTEIN (g): 3.7
CARBS (g): 12.4
FIBRE (g): 6.5
CALORIES: 229
SERVES: 1

We all know that we should be eating more leafy greens. Not only are they loaded with minerals, vitamins, fibre and phytochemicals, but they also enhance digestion. However, it can get a little boring eating salads day after day, which is why I love the odd green smoothie. I aim for 2–3 smoothies a week, although there's nothing wrong with having one every day. Lots of our customers come in for a classic green smoothie every morning with a scoop of protein added to boost their macros. I must have tried over 100 green smoothies and this one is not only delicious, it also contains less fruit than many.

MY GO-TO CLASSIC GREEN SMOOTHIE

1 handful of de-stemmed kale or spinach
½ ripe avocado
1cm piece of fresh root ginger, peeled
½ apple or pear, cored
100ml coconut water
100ml water
1 tsp chia seeds
10g peanut butter (optional)
1 tbsp greens powder or a scoop of protein powder

Simply blend all the ingredients in a high-speed blender until completely smooth. If you like a colder smoothie, add ice. If you add protein, greens powder or nut butter, remember to adjust the macros.

NOTE

Wrap the other half of the apple or pear in clingfilm and pop it in the fridge for the next day's smoothie.

I use a mixed greens powder in this smoothie, which contains lots of different ingredients.

FRITTERS, 3 WAYS

COURGETTE FRITTERS

FAT (g): 4.4
PROTEIN (g): 6.6
CARBS (g): 22.7
FIBRE (g): 1.8
CALORIES: 160
SERVES: 2 (MAKES 4 FRITTERS)

1 large courgette, grated
50g gluten-free flour or plain flour
½ tsp baking powder
good pinch of salt and pepper
pinch of dried red chilli flakes
1 egg, beaten
1 small garlic clove, finely chopped
2 spring onions, finely chopped
a few tbsp finely chopped coriander
1 tsp coconut oil or low-cal fry spray, for frying

Place the grated courgette in a tea towel or kitchen paper and squeeze well. You want it as dry as possible. Place the courgette in a bowl, add the remaining ingredients, except the oil, and mix thoroughly.

Heat a large frying pan over a high heat and add a little coconut oil or low-cal spray. Place a large spoonful of the fritter mixture (equal to 2 tbsp) into the pan and repeat to make 4 fritters. Turn the heat down to medium-high.

Cook for 2–3 minutes until golden brown, then turn them over and cook for a minute on the other side. You may need to adjust the cooking temperature to medium. Remove the fritters and drain on kitchen paper to remove any excess oil. Serve the fritters hot.

SWEETCORN FRITTERS

FAT (g): 6.3
PROTEIN (g): 8.6
CARBS (g): 43.8
FIBRE (g): 5
CALORIES: 276
SERVES: 2 (MAKES 4 FRITTERS)

250g canned sweetcorn, rinsed and drained
2 spring onions, roughly chopped
1 egg, lightly beaten
1 garlic clove
1 chilli, deseeded if liked
1 small bunch of coriander – leaves and stems
pinch of salt and a grind of black pepper
65g gluten-free flour
½ tsp baking powder
finely grated zest of 1 lemon
1 tsp coconut oil or low-cal fry spray, for frying

Place three-quarters of the sweetcorn, the spring onions, egg, garlic, chilli, coriander, salt and pepper in a blender or mini chopper and whizz until smooth, then stir in the flour, baking powder, lemon zest and the remaining corn.

Heat a little oil in a frying pan over a medium-high heat. When hot, drop 2 heaped tbsp of mixture per fritter into the pan and cook for 2 minutes on each side, or until golden. Remove and drain on kitchen paper. Serve the fritters hot.

SWEET POTATO HASHIES

FAT (g): 5.9
PROTEIN (g): 2
CARBS (g): 29.7
FIBRE (g): 3.1
CALORIES: 186
SERVES: 2 (MAKES 4 FRITTERS)

1 medium/large sweet potato, peeled and
   coarsely grated
½ small onion, thinly sliced
30g gluten-free flour
1 garlic clove, grated
1 egg, lightly beaten
pinch of salt and pepper
1 tsp coconut oil or low-cal fry spray, for frying

Place the sweet potato in a colander and rinse in plenty of cold water, then dry in a clean tea towel and wring out really hard. The sweet potato needs to be super dry. Tip into a bowl, add the onion, garlic, flour, egg, salt and pepper and mix well.

Heat a little oil in a frying pan over a medium-high heat. When hot, drop 2 tbsp of the mixture per fritter into the pan and use a spatula to flatten them out. Cook for 3 minutes, then flip over and cook for a further 2 minutes until deep golden and crisp. Remove and drain on kitchen paper. Serve the hashies hot.

GREEN GODDESS DIP

FAT (g): 11.2
PROTEIN (g): 0.7
CARBS (g): 0.4
FIBRE (g): 0.8
CALORIES: 107
SERVES: 6

1 bunch of watercress
1 bunch of herbs of choice
2 spring onions
finely grated zest and juice of 2 lemons
1 tbsp capers (optional)
1 tbsp cornichons (optional)
6 tbsp extra virgin olive oil
2 tbsp water
salt and pepper
½ garlic clove

Blend all the ingredients together in a blender or food processor. Alternatively, chop everything roughly if you prefer a chunkier sauce. Serve.

Fritters are bang on trend right now. They are the new avocado-on-toast and are so simple to make. These are my go-to weekend breakfast when I have a little more time in the kitchen. Here are my three favourites – all amazing topped with a soft poached egg or a quick tomato salad with some good-quality balsamic vinegar and a handful of your favourite salad leaves. Alternatively, try them with the Spicy Avocado Dip from page 80, the raita from page 87, or the Green Goddess Dip above.

FAT (g): 22.8
PROTEIN (g): 17.4
CARBS (g): 23.2
FIBRE (g): 7.3
CALORIES: 382
SERVES: 2

You can vary the spices and veggies in this one-pot wonder to suit your palate and it is wonderful when served with crusty bread for a lazy weekend brunch or even a light evening meal. This dish is largely made up of ingredients commonly found in your kitchen and fridge and it's high in protein, fibre and healthy fats, too.

> "If you have the calorie allowance, you can add a little sautéed chorizo, but no more than 40g."

ONE-POT BRUNCH (SHAKSHUKA)

2 tbsp olive oil
1 onion, thinly sliced
1 tsp cumin seeds
½ tsp smoked paprika
pinch of saffron threads (optional)
pinch of cayenne pepper or dried red chilli flakes (optional)
2 red peppers, sliced
1 tsp honey
2 thyme sprigs, leaves picked and roughly chopped (or use dried)
400g can good-quality chopped tomatoes
salt and pepper
4 eggs
a few leaves of flat leaf parsley and/or coriander, roughly chopped, to garnish

Preheat the oven to 200°C/gas mark 6. Place 2 ovenproof serving dishes on a baking tray.

Heat the oil in a large frying pan over a medium heat, add the onion and sauté for 10 minutes. Increase the heat and add the cumin, smoked paprika, saffron and cayenne or chilli, if using. Stir constantly for a minute so the spices release their flavours but don't burn, then add the peppers, honey, thyme, tomatoes, salt and pepper. Reduce the heat to low and cook for 15 minutes until thickened.

Divide the mixture between the serving dishes, then break 2 eggs into each dish, pouring the eggs into the gaps in the mixture. Sprinkle with salt, cover with foil and cook in the oven for 10–12 minutes, or until the egg just sets.

Sprinkle the chopped herbs over the top and serve immediately.

NOTE

Instead of using fresh red pepper, try adding the ready-roasted jarred ones you find in the supermarket instead.

FAT (g): 19
PROTEIN (g): 13
CARBS (g): 25.4
FIBRE (g): 4.9
CALORIES: 352
SERVES: 2 (MAKES 4 PANCAKES)

Teff is a high-prebiotic fibre whole grain and is a good source of protein, manganese, iron and calcium, which means that it's useful as a healthy weight-managing and bone-strengthening food. The sweet dukkah is a simple way to catapult omega-3 fatty acids, plant-based protein, vitamins, minerals and fibre into your diet. I sprinkle it over salads, breakfasts, smoothies and desserts.

TEFF PANCAKES WITH SWEET DUKKAH & FRUIT COMPOTE

65g teff flour
¼ tsp baking powder
1 tsp coconut sugar
pinch of salt
1 egg
1 tsp vanilla extract (optional)
100ml milk of choice
1 tbsp coconut oil or butter, for frying
2 tbsp Greek yogurt, natural live yogurt or coconut yogurt, to serve
4 tbsp fruit compote of choice

For the sweet dukkah
50g pistachios
50g flaxseeds
50g sunflower seeds
50g almonds
50g hazelnuts
2 tsp each black and white sesame seeds
2 tbsp coconut sugar
1 tsp ground cinnamon

For the sweet dukkah, using a high-speed food processor, blend all of the ingredients to a medium consistency. Store in an airtight container in the fridge for up to 2 months.

To make the pancakes, sift all the dry ingredients together into a large bowl. In a separate bowl, whisk the egg, vanilla, if using, and milk together until combined. Add the egg mixture to the flour mixture and stir until a smooth batter forms. Leave to rest at room temperature for 5 minutes.

Heat one-quarter of the oil or butter in a frying pan over a medium heat. When hot, add one-quarter of the batter to the pan and cook for 1–2 minutes on each side, or until golden and small bubbles appear on the surface. Remove from the pan and keep warm while you make the other pancakes. Serve with a dollop of yogurt, 2 tbsp compote of your choice and 1 tbsp of the sweet dukkah.

FRUIT COMPOTE

Fruit compotes have a bad reputation for being full of added sugars, but extra refined sugar isn't necessary, as the sweetness comes from the fresh seasonal fruit. Here are my favourites, which I serve with all kinds of desserts and breakfast dishes. For all of them, put the fruit in a pan with 50ml water, 1 tsp natural sweetener of choice, 1 tsp vanilla extract and a pinch of spice if you like. Simmer for 5 minutes.

Grated apple & raspberry
Mixed red berries with orange zest
Grated pear & apple (plus a little rosewater – divine)
Blueberries & grated apple

FAT (g): 26.7
PROTEIN (g): 20.3
CARBS (g): 41.2
FIBRE (g): 16.3
CALORIES: 519
SERVES: 2

This is my lazy Sunday go-to breakfast. It's a perfectly balanced dish with healthy fats, protein from a variety of sources, veggies and slow-release carbohydrates. Pimp it with bacon, turkey bacon, steamed kale, sautéed spinach – the tweaks are endless.

HUEVOS RANCHEROS WITH WHOLEMEAL TORTILLA

"These are absolutely banging wrapped up as breakfast burritos."

200g canned black beans, drained
50ml water
1 tsp smoked paprika
1 tsp butter
1 tsp ground cumin
½ garlic clove, crushed
1 tsp salt
2 eggs
2 wholemeal tortillas
2 tsp low-sugar chipotle sauce or your favourite hot sauce

For the guacamole
1 medium avocado
juice of 1 lime
¼ red onion, finely diced
½ tsp dried red chilli flakes, or to taste
1 small bunch of coriander, finely chopped
1 small handful of cherry tomatoes, quartered

First, cook the beans. Place the beans and water in a saucepan with the smoked paprika, butter, cumin, garlic and salt, and simmer over a low heat for 10 minutes. Remove from the heat and mash or blend until you get a texture you like – I like it chunky.

Meanwhile, make the guacamole. In a bowl, mash the avocado with the lime juice, onion, chilli flakes and half the coriander, then stir in the tomatoes. Set aside.

Fry the eggs to your liking while you plate up the rest of the dish.

Toast or warm the tortillas, then add half the beans to each tortilla, top with the guacamole, a fried egg, the chipotle sauce and more coriander and serve immediately.

LUNCH OR DINNER... IT'S ALL GOOD!

I've combined afternoon and evening eating in this chapter to allow flexibility, as some people like a large lunch and a small dinner, whereas others prefer to eat a large meal in the evening.

For me it depends on what kind of day I've had, whether I've trained and what plans I have in the evening. I don't want to create barriers to eating healthily and losing weight by telling you what to eat and at what times, so by putting them together you can pick and choose.

Feel free to add lean protein to the salads, but don't forget to add the macros to your daily total. These meals are quick, tasty, affordable dishes you can whip up with basic ingredients and, in most cases, in less than 15 minutes, so you don't have to spend ages in the kitchen.

FAT (g): 30.6
PROTEIN (g): 64.9
CARBS (g): 27
FIBRE (g): 18.9
CALORIES: 681
SERVES: 1

The volumetric diet is based around the principles of eating large portions of high-volume, low-calorie food to help you feel fuller quicker and for longer, therefore consuming fewer calories. Volumetric relies on foods with a low-energy density and high water content, such as fruits and vegetables. It is paired here with lean protein.

AMAZING VOLUMETRIC TURKEY SALAD

200g turkey breast, thinly sliced
1 tsp low-salt chicken seasoning or spices of your choice, such as smoked paprika, oregano, harissa, cumin, turmeric, garam masala
1 tsp olive oil

For the salad
1 whole head of romaine lettuce, chopped
2 cooked beetroot, chopped
a few cherry tomatoes, chopped
1 carrot, coarsely grated
½ cucumber, grated or thinly sliced
6 lightly steamed Tenderstem broccoli florets, or asparagus if it's in season

For the dressing
juice of 1 lemon
1 tbsp water
1 tbsp extra virgin olive oil
2 spring onions
salt and pepper
½ garlic clove
pinch of dried red chilli flakes (optional)

To finish
few handfuls of herbs of choice, such as parsley, mint and coriander, stalks separated and reserved for the dressing and leaves roughly chopped
20g toasted walnuts OR 50g reduced-fat cheese, grated

Marinate the turkey breast in the seasoning or spices. This can be done about 1 hour in advance in a shallow bowl in the fridge, or at the last minute before cooking.

Heat a griddle pan or grill until hot, grease with the olive oil, then cook the turkey over a medium-high heat for 4 minutes on each side or until cooked all the way through.

For the salad, simply toss all the ingredients together in a large bowl.

To make the dressing, simply whizz all the ingredients including the reserved herb stalks together in a blender or mini chopper, then pour over the salad and toss through until coated.

Top the salad with the turkey breast and scatter over the chopped herbs, nuts or cheese.

FAT (g): 21.9
PROTEIN (g): 10.1
CARBS (g): 23.4
FIBRE (g): 11.7
CALORIES: 354
MAKES: 4 PORTIONS

This colourful raw salad takes minutes to make. The dressing is punchy and fresh and is full of healthy fats from the nuts. Unlike some of the salads in this section this one needs to be dressed JUST before serving to maintain the crunch.

ASIAN RAW SLAW & GINGER SALAD WITH TOASTED CASHEWS

½ red cabbage
½ white cabbage
4 raw beetroot
4 medium carrots
2 peppers (any colour)
1 small bunch each of coriander and mint
100g cashew nuts, chopped
2 tbsp sesame seeds, lightly toasted

> "Make double the amount of dressing and store in a jam jar in the fridge for up to 1 week."

For the dressing
2 tbsp soy sauce or tamari
2 tbsp toasted sesame oil
2 tbsp water
5cm piece of fresh root ginger, peeled and grated
1 spring onion, finely sliced
½ tsp dried red chilli flakes, or to taste
juice of 2 limes

Finely shred the cabbages, then julienne, spiralize or simply grate the beetroot and carrots. Slice the peppers and finely chop the herbs, then place everything in a large bowl with all the remaining salad ingredients and toss together.

To make the dressing, whisk all the ingredients together in a small bowl or place in a jam jar, cover with a lid and shake until combined. If you prefer a smoother dressing, whizz in a blender.

Heat a dry frying pan over medium heat and, when hot, toast the cashew nuts for a couple of minutes to develop their flavour.

Just before serving pour the dressing over the salad and toss well.

FAT (g): 22.2
PROTEIN (g): 9.5
CARBS (g): 18.4
FIBRE (g): 9.2
CALORIES: 330
SERVES: 4

This is summer feel-good food at its finest and a great way to help you get to your 5-a-day, with lots of flavour from a delicious lower oil dressing. If you choose quinoa, make a little extra and reserve 80g for the Prawn, Courgette & Quinoa Patties on page 122.

JEWELLED TABBOULEH WITH HARISSA ROAST AUBERGINE

1 aubergine, diced
salt
2 tbsp harissa paste
100g cooked quinoa (or bulgur wheat or buckwheat [higher carb], or 1 medium cauliflower, coarsely grated [low carb])
1 cucumber, diced
1 small punnet of cherry tomatoes (about 330g), chopped
selection of herbs, such as mint, coriander and parsley, roughly chopped
1 large red pepper, diced
2 handfuls of kale, stalks removed and leaves roughly chopped
4 tbsp flaked almonds, lightly toasted (pistachios or pine nuts work well here too)
seeds of 1 small pomegranate
2 tbsp seeds of choice, such as toasted pumpkin seeds

For the dressing
2 spring onions, finely sliced
stalks of all the herbs you used, except mint as they are very woody
finely grated zest and juice of 2 lemons (or try orange and lime)
1 tsp salt
good grind of black pepper
1 tsp smoked paprika
pinch of ground cinnamon (optional)
1 tsp cumin (if it's the seeds, toast them in a dry pan first)
4 tbsp extra virgin olive oil
2 tbsp water

Preheat the oven to 200°C/gas mark 6.

Start with the aubergine. Sprinkle a little salt over the aubergine dice in a colander and leave for 10 minutes. This isn't essential but it removes the bitterness and excess moisture before cooking. After 10 minutes, pat the aubergine dry and brush or rub all over with the harissa paste. Scatter the aubergine on a baking tray and roast in the oven for about 20–30 minutes, until golden.

For the dressing, simply whizz all the ingredients in a blender until the herb stalks have broken down. Alternatively, just leave the herb stalks out and whisk everything together in a small bowl with a fork.

Place the aubergine and all the remaining ingredients in a large bowl and toss through the dressing. You can either dress the whole salad at once or portion the salad out and add the dressing to a jar to dress as you go. It is fine to dress the salad in advance as the flavours mingle and the acidity in the lemon helps break the kale down, too. This salad keeps in the fridge for 2–3 days.

FAT (g): 3
PROTEIN (g): 5.6
CARBS (g): 10.6
FIBRE (g): 1.8
CALORIES: 95
MAKES: 4

I make a batch of these crêpes one evening a week and use them for lunches as a healthier alternative to sandwiches. You can either top them or stuff them and roll them with some of my favourite variations below. The crêpes freeze well, but make sure you separate them with baking paper before freezing so they are easier to defrost.

"The nutritional breakdown given here is just for 1 crêpe, cooked in coconut oil. Look up the extra macros online for whichever toppings you choose."

SPELT & SPINACH CRÊPES WITH LOADS OF TOPPINGS

60g spelt or buckwheat flour
1 egg
80g baby spinach leaves
150ml milk of choice
good grind of salt and pepper
1 tsp coconut oil or low-cal fry spray, for frying

For the toppings
½ ripe avocado and 75g smoked salmon
½ ripe avocado and 100g shredded cooked chicken breast
2 tbsp guacamole (see page 58) and a fried egg (make it boiled if you're eating on the go)
fat slices of beef tomato, a few olives, finely diced red onion, diced cucumber and 50g crumbled feta

Put the flour, egg, spinach leaves, milk, salt and pepper in a food processor and blend until smooth.

Heat the coconut oil or a little low-cal fry spray in a non-stick frying pan. When hot, add one-quarter of the batter, circulating the pan to keep the crêpe round, and cook for 2–3 minutes on each side, flipping it over when the crêpe starts to come away from the pan. Remove from the pan and repeat with the rest of the batter to make 3 more crêpes. Add a topping and serve. They are delicious hot or cold.

FAT (g): 20.6
PROTEIN (g): 18.4
CARBS (g): 46.8
FIBRE (g): 20.7
CALORIES: 488
SERVES: 2 (MAKES 4 TACOS)

Popular on a detox diet, this dish was a winner on the TV show where we made our own tacos with chickpea flour. It's a bit time-consuming, so as corn tortillas are gluten free and readily available, I've used them in this recipe for convenience. You can buy sprouted seeds from health-food shops. They add a good flavour, but aren't essential. This is one of those recipes where you don't even notice it is vegetarian – meat-free Mondays never looked so good! The beans are delicious hot or cold and keep for a week in the fridge. They are amazing as a dip for crudités.

BLACK BEAN & COURGETTE TACOS WITH MANGO MELON SALSA

4 small corn tortillas

For the filling
400g can black beans, drained
1 bunch of coriander, stalks and leaves separated, leaves chopped
salt and pepper
1 small garlic clove, crushed
1 large courgette, cut in half, then into thick strips
1 tsp olive oil, for frying

For the salsa
80g melon of choice, such as honeydew or watermelon, peeled and cut into 1cm cubes
80g mango, peeled and cut into 1cm cubes
½ cucumber, cut into 1cm cubes
1 spring onion, thinly sliced
finely grated zest and juice of 1 lime

To serve
1 medium ripe avocado, sliced
sprouted seeds (optional)

Heat the beans with the coriander stalks, a little salt and pepper and the garlic in a saucepan over a low-medium heat until simmering, about 5–10 minutes. Remove from the heat and whizz in a blender until smooth. Alternatively, mash the mixture, but if mashing leave the stalks out as they don't get broken down. Reserve.

Heat a griddle pan over a high heat until hot. Lightly brush the courgette strips with the oil, add to the pan and fry until golden char marks appear.

For the salsa, simply mix everything together in a bowl with half of the coriander leaves and keep in the fridge until ready to serve.

Toast the corn tortillas or warm through, however you like them.

When you're ready to serve, dollop one-quarter of the black beans on each warmed taco. Top with the griddled courgettes and a generous spoonful of the salsa. Finally, top with slices of avocado, a little sprinkle of the remaining coriander leaves and sprouted seeds, if using.

FAT (g): 32.4
PROTEIN (g): 9.4
CARBS (g): 22.7
FIBRE (g): 7
CALORIES: 434
SERVES: 2

Here, I give two healthier variations on this classic Italian dish. The pasta is swapped for griddled courgette, giving the same pasta consistency but saving you 35g carbs and 150 calories per person. Of course, if you can't be bothered with slicing and stuffing the courgettes simply spiralize them, then toss in the pesto and tomato sauce. This is delicious eaten either hot or cold, and can be served with a green side salad if you're particularly hungry.

COURGETTE CANNELLONI

2–3 medium courgettes, thinly sliced lengthways
1 tsp olive oil
salt and pepper

For the pesto
1 large bunch of basil
50g Parmesan cheese (optional), chopped
20g pine nuts, lightly toasted in a dry frying pan
4 tbsp extra virgin olive oil
4 tbsp water
juice of 1 lemon
salt and pepper
1 garlic clove, roughly chopped

For the marinara sauce
½ tsp olive oil or low-cal fry spray
1 small onion, thinly sliced
680g jar of best-quality tomato passata
1 tsp dried oregano

First, make the pesto. Simply whizz all the ingredients in a mini chopper or blender until it's the texture you like. Don't be tempted to add more oil, as each tablespoon is 120 calories (as a comparison, a full-on iced doughnut is about 180 calories…). Just drip in some water or lemon juice if you need to, but it should be quite thick.

For the marinara sauce, heat the oil or low-cal fry spray in a saucepan over a low-medium heat and sauté the onion for at least 8 minutes until soft. Increase the heat, add the passata and oregano and simmer for about 10 minutes until thickened. Season, then remove from the heat.

Heat a griddle pan over a medium-high heat until hot. Brush the courgette slices with the oil, sprinkle with salt and pepper and griddle for 2–3 minutes on each side until char marks appear. Remove the courgette and drain on kitchen paper.

When ready to serve, add about a tablespoon of the pesto to each courgette strip (about 8 in total), spread, and roll up the courgette but not too tightly. Spoon the sauce on each serving plate, then place 4 courgette cannelloni on top to serve.

MEAT VARIATION

Sauté 1 small, thinly sliced onion in ½ tsp olive oil, then increase the heat, add 2 chopped slices of bacon and 200g lean steak mince and cook until the meat is coloured, about 5 minutes. Add a 680g jar of best-quality tomato passata and 1 tsp dried oregano and simmer for 20 minutes or until the meat is tender. Season.

Nutritional breakdown: fat 36.6g; protein 31.2g; carbs 22.7g; fibre 7g; calories 559.

FAT (g): 4.7
PROTEIN (g): 23.4
CARBS (g): 33.1
FIBRE (g): 2.6
CALORIES: 273
SERVES: 2 (MAKES 6 FRITTERS)

Canned tuna is an amazing protein source and really inexpensive, too. There are only 100 calories in 24g protein, making it my go-to tasty, healthy, low-carb, high-protein meal. The fact that these fritters take less than 15 minutes to make and can be frozen is a bonus. These are a great lunch or snack for me when I'm in a hurry. Serve with the Spicy Avocado Dip from page 80, if you like.

> **"Replace the tuna with flaked salmon if you want to increase the omega-3 fatty acids."**

TUNA & COURGETTE FRITTERS

1 small courgette, grated
120g can tuna, drained
½ small bunch of chives, coriander or parsley (whichever fresh herb you have to hand), finely chopped
80g wholemeal self-raising flour or gluten-free flour
finely grated zest of 1 lemon
salt and pepper
1 egg, beaten
about 80ml milk of choice
1 tsp olive oil or low-cal fry spray, for frying

To serve
Spicy Avocado Dip (see page 80)
green leafy salad

Place the grated courgette on a sheet of kitchen paper and gently scrunch together to draw out any excess moisture.

Place the courgette in a bowl with the tuna and herbs and mix to flake the tuna. Add the flour, lemon zest and seasoning to taste, then stir in the beaten egg and enough milk to form a thick batter.

Heat the olive oil or low-cal fry spray in a frying pan over a medium-high heat. When hot, spoon in 2 tbsp of the batter per fritter into the pan and fry for 3 minutes, or until golden brown. Flip over and cook the other side for a further 3 minutes until golden brown and crispy. You can make 3 fritters in one batch. Remove and keep warm while you cook the remaining 3 fritters.

If not eating immediately, allow the fritters to cool before freezing for up to 1 month. Serve with the Spicy Avocado Dip and a green leafy salad for a light lunch.

FAT (g): 32.3
PROTEIN (g): 32.9
CARBS (g): 21.8
FIBRE (g): 3.9
CALORIES: 517
SERVES: 2

I know this is a classic breakfast dish but I've never been able to eat pungent fish for breakfast since I watched my Granda Ernie get through 20 kippers every morning when I was a kid. I much prefer it for lunch or dinner. I've switched up the traditional rice for brown basmati, and haddock for mackerel, which is high in vitamin D, some B vitamins, selenium and a rich source of omega-3 fatty acids. I've also added some extra healing spices and veggies, too.

MACKEREL BROWN RICE KEDGEREE

50g brown basmati rice
150ml boiling water
salt and pepper
1 tsp olive oil
½ white onion, thinly sliced
1 tsp mustard seeds
1 tsp ground turmeric
pinch of chilli powder (optional)
2 large handfuls of kale, stalks removed and
    leaves chopped
200g smoked mackerel, flaked
2 hard-boiled eggs, quartered
1 small handful of parsley, finely chopped, to garnish

Place the rice in a saucepan, add the boiling water and a pinch of salt, cover with a lid and simmer over a very low heat for 20 minutes.

Meanwhile, heat the oil in another pan over a medium-low heat and fry the onion for about 8 minutes, or until softened. Increase the heat, add the mustard seeds, turmeric, chilli powder and kale and stir until everything is coated. Keep the heat high for a minute or so, season with salt and pepper and then throw in the flaked mackerel. Take off the heat and wait for the rice, if necessary.

After 20 minutes, tip the rice and any cooking water into the mackerel pan. Stir well, cover with a lid and simmer over a low heat for a further 5–10 minutes until the rice is cooked. Uncover and allow any excess moisture to evaporate before spooning into 2 serving bowls and topping with a hard-boiled egg and herbs.

FAT (g): 12.6
PROTEIN (g): 7.5
CARBS (g): 25.1
FIBRE (g): 13.3
CALORIES: 271
SERVES: 2

Another classic from my Eat Naked café, this salad is bursting full of flavour and vitamin C. It is great served with pitta breads and hummus for an exotic lunch. The longer this salad sits, the better the flavours become, so leftovers are a godsend.

MOROCCAN SESAME CARROT SALAD

4 medium carrots, julienned, coarsely grated or spiralized
1 small bunch of coriander, parsley and mint or any combination of the three
1 tsp cumin seeds, lightly toasted
1 tsp smoked paprika
finely grated zest and juice of 1 orange
1 tbsp harissa paste
seeds of 1 small pomegranate
1 tsp black sesame seeds or another seed of choice
4 tbsp flaked almonds, lightly toasted

Simply throw all the ingredients, except the sesame seeds and flaked almonds, together in a big bowl and give it a good massage. Top with the seeds and almonds and serve.

FAT (g): 13.3
PROTEIN (g): 29.1
CARBS (g): 15
FIBRE (g): 2.8
CALORIES: 302
SERVES: 2

This recipe is inspired by the 5-factor diet from the TV show, which promises weight loss by preparing meals in 5 minutes, with 5 ingredients and eating 5 times a day. I love the promotion of balance in this diet: protein, complex carbs, fibre and good fats in every meal. The cucumber salad in this is a winner as it contains no fat.

SALMON WITH CHEAT'S CREAMY CUCUMBER & DILL SALAD

2 x 200g salmon fillets, skin removed, if you prefer
2 slices of lemon
salt and pepper
160g new potatoes with skins, halved unless small
1 cucumber, halved lengthways, watery seeds scraped out and thinly sliced
2 tbsp chopped dill
finely grated zest and juice of 1 lemon
1 tsp smoked paprika (optional)
100g no-fat soured cream or Greek yogurt

> "Most supermarkets sell ready-to-eat poached salmon fillets if you don't feel confident cooking fish."

Preheat the oven to 200°C/gas mark 6 and line a baking tray with foil.

Place the salmon on the prepared baking tray with a slice of lemon on top and a good grind of salt and pepper and cook in the oven for 12–15 minutes. You can pop your potatoes in 10 minutes before (drizzled with 1 tsp olive oil and sprinkled with sea salt) and leave them in to roast with the salmon or you can steam them for 20–25 minutes until tender.

Meanwhile, make the salad. Toss the cucumber, dill, lemon zest and juice, smoked paprika, if using, salt and pepper and the soured cream or yogurt together in a large bowl.

Serve the salmon and potatoes hot for a comforting dinner or cold for a picnic-style lunch, along with the salad.

FAT (g): 15.9
PROTEIN (g): 39.3
CARBS (g): 11.6
FIBRE (g): 5.8
CALORIES: 359
SERVES: 2

This is a recipe from the TV show and is based around intuitive eating, making food choices without guilt and completely enjoying the process of eating. It helps to develop a better relationship with food and eventually make better choices. I was an intuitive eater when I lost my weight and this is the kind of thing I enjoyed either before the gym, or with 180g cooked brown basmati rice after the gym. This dish is also wonderful doubled up and served family-style on a platter at a barbecue or picnic.

CRUNCHY-PUNCHY VIETNAMESE BEEF SALAD

300g very fresh fillet steak (it needs to be very good quality, as you won't be cooking it), finely sliced

For the marinade
juice of 2 limes
1 tbsp water
1 tbsp fish sauce
1 tbsp soy sauce or tamari
1 tsp toasted sesame oil
2 spring onions, roughly chopped
1 lemongrass stalk, chopped, or 1 tbsp fresh lemongrass paste
1 garlic clove, grated
2.5cm piece of fresh root ginger, peeled and grated or 1 tbsp fresh ginger paste

For the salad
1 small bunch of coriander and/or mint, roughly chopped
2 baby gem lettuces, roughly chopped
2 handfuls of beansprouts
½ cucumber, julienned or finely ribboned with a vegetable peeler
1 carrot, julienned or spiralized
2 tbsp peanuts, roughly chopped

First, make the marinade. Whizz all the ingredients in a blender or mini chopper. Alternatively, simply whisk all the ingredients together in a bowl, then grate in the garlic and ginger.

Place the steak in a dish, pour over the marinade and marinate for at least 5–10 minutes. You can marinate it overnight in the fridge, in a bowl covered with clingfilm. The longer the steak is left the more it will 'cook' in the marinade.

When ready to serve, place all the salad ingredients, except the peanuts, in a large bowl. Drain the meat from the marinade, reserving any excess marinade, and toss through the salad. Top with the peanuts and some of the reserved marinade, if you like.

FAT (g): 15
PROTEIN (g): 37.8
CARBS (g): 5.6
FIBRE (g): 4.1
CALORIES: 317
SERVES: 2 (MAKES 6 CUPS)

This is something I eat several times a week as it's so delicious and super low-calorie. The dips themselves are versatile and you can add them to lots of other dishes. This dish is a powerhouse of lean protein, fibre and healthy fats. I've kept the turkey mince simple as the dips have a lot of punchy flavours.

TURKEY MINCE LETTUCE CUPS WITH SPICY AVOCADO DIP & TOMATO SALSA

300g turkey mince
1 tbsp chipotle sauce
pinch of smoked paprika (optional)
2 tbsp water
salt and pepper
2 baby gem lettuces, stalks cut off and the best 6 largest leaves picked, inner leaves kept for another salad

For the spicy avocado dip
1 large ripe avocado
finely grated zest and juice of 1 lime
1 tbsp extra virgin olive oil
1 tbsp water
2 tbsp Greek yogurt
1 spring onion or ¼ red onion, roughly chopped
½ garlic clove, roughly chopped
salt and pepper
½ tsp dried red chilli flakes or fresh chilli

For the tomato salsa
4 good-quality vine-ripened tomatoes
¼ onion, diced (optional)
juice of 1 lime
1 small handful of coriander, finely chopped
salt and pepper

Heat a frying pan over a high heat until hot, then add the turkey mince and cook until browned all over, about 5 minutes. Add the remaining ingredients, except the lettuce, cover with a lid, reduce the heat and simmer for 20 minutes, adding a little more water if the sauce becomes too dry. Season to taste.

Meanwhile, make the dips. Blend all the ingredients for the spicy avocado dip in a blender or food processor until smooth. It should be unctuous like a yogurt consistency. Set aside in the fridge.

For the tomato salsa, cut the tomatoes in half, scoop out the seeds and cut the flesh into dice. Place in a bowl with the onion, if using. Add the lime juice, stir in the coriander and finish with a good pinch of salt and grind of black pepper. Allow to stand at room temperature for as long as you have, to allow the flavours to develop.

When you're ready to serve, arrange the lettuce cups on a serving plate and fill with the turkey mince, then top with the salsa. Either dip the boats into the avocado dip or spoon it over the boats before eating.

FAT (g): 15.9
PROTEIN (g): 56.2
CARBS (g): 14
FIBRE (g): 4.9
CALORIES: 436
SERVES: 3

When I first tried these on the TV show I was so sceptical – cauliflower as a binding agent in meatballs? But the cauliflower reduces the carbs to practically nothing while keeping the fibre and contributing towards your 5-a-day, and they are baked too, so are much healthier than fried. Freezing these is a top tip, so this recipe is for six portions – two to have now, and four to freeze. They are also good on their own, or with courgetti for a low-carb meal.

HERBY LOW-CARB MEATBALLS IN MARINARA

> "Don't be tempted to load up with more cheese – a few herbs and chilli flakes are excellent garnishes with no calories added."

low-cal fry spray or a little oil for the tin
1 medium cauliflower, cut into florets
600g lean beef mince
50g Parmesan cheese, grated
1 small bunch of basil and/or parsley, finely chopped, plus extra to serve
1 tsp dried oregano
1 tsp smoked paprika
salt and pepper
1 garlic clove, crushed or grated
1 egg, beaten
½ red onion, very finely diced
½ quantity hot marinara sauce recipe (see page 70)

Preheat the oven to 200°C/gas mark 6 and line a large baking tin or ovenproof dish with foil, then spray with low-cal fry spray or rub with a tiny amount of oil, just to stop the meatballs sticking.

Grate the cauliflower or pulse in a food processor until it resembles rice, then transfer to a large bowl. Add the remaining ingredients and scrunch together with your hands to combine. Alternatively, remove the cauliflower from the food processor, tip the rest of the ingredients except the sauce into the processor and blend to combine, then scrunch through the cauliflower in the bowl.

Using your hands, roll the mixture into 21 balls, about 5cm in diameter, and place in the prepared tin in a single layer. Bake in the oven for 20 minutes until golden and browned all over. Serve with the marinara sauce and some basil.

FAT (g): 19.2
PROTEIN (g): 47.7
CARBS (g): 26.8
FIBRE (g): 13.4
CALORIES: 498
SERVES: 2

This is a great idea for leftover lamb from your Sunday lunch. Here, it is transformed into a stand-out meal in its own right and is paired with fibre-rich beans layered with lots of flavours. The three-bean smash is also amazing with crudités, so double it up for lunches and snacks through the week.

MONDAY'S CRISPY LAMB WITH LEMONY THREE-BEAN SMASH & LOTS OF HERBS

5g butter or coconut oil
1 tbsp rose harissa (paste or powder is fine)
250g leftover roast lamb, pulled or shredded if it's shoulder and chopped if it's leg
1 small garlic clove, crushed
400g canned white beans, such as flageolet, cannellini or butter beans (mix them or just one type)
salt and pepper
finely grated zest and juice of 1 lemon
1 small bunch of mint and/or parsley, finely chopped, to garnish

Heat a frying pan over a high heat until hot, add the butter or oil and harissa, then immediately add the lamb and toss to coat in the buttery spices. Leave the lamb over a high heat until hot and as crispy as you like it, about 5 minutes. Transfer the lamb to a plate and reserve.

Throw the garlic and beans into the pan and again leave over a high heat so the beans mop up the lamb juices and catch a little. They will start to break down, so you can either crush with a fork or leave them whole. If the mix is drier than you like, add a little water. Check for seasoning, then add the lemon zest and juice and give the pan one final shake.

Serve the bean smash immediately with the lamb piled high on top and garnished with the chopped herbs. If you have the calories, a little flatbread with this is delicious.

FAT (g): 4.7
PROTEIN (g): 18.5
CARBS (g): 69.6
FIBRE (g): 11.1
CALORIES: 417
SERVES: 4

The flavours in this are unbelievable – it's one of those dishes I will make again and again and eat in some form every day, hot or cold, in wraps, with any leftover meat as a side for curry and on its own. This needs to be done from scratch so no cheating with shop-bought or canned lentils. My nana Perveen has been making me this for years and adds toasted flaked almonds and dried fruits, but that's a little decadent here.

NORTH AFRICAN LENTILS WITH SWEET ONIONS (MUJADARA)

250g brown lentils, rinsed
1 tsp coconut oil or low-cal fry spray
2 tsp cumin seeds
2 tsp ground coriander
1 tsp mixed spice
1 tsp ground cinnamon
2 tsp ground turmeric
200g white basmati rice
salt and pepper
350ml water

For the sweet onions
1 tsp olive oil
5g butter
2 onions, thinly sliced
salt
1 tsp honey

To serve
natural yogurt
coriander or parsley or mint, or a mix of all three, roughly chopped
lemon wedges

First, prepare the sweet onions. Heat the olive oil and butter in a large pan over a high heat until bubbling. Throw in the onions, stir to coat and reduce the heat to medium. Add 1 tsp salt (this draws out the moisture from the onions and help them caramelize), then cover the pan and cook over a medium-high heat for 15 minutes. Add the honey, stir and cook, uncovered, for a further 5–10 minutes until golden, sticky and caramelized.

Pop the lentils into a saucepan, cover with plenty of water, bring to the boil, then reduce the heat and simmer for 10 minutes. Drain, reserving the water.

Heat the coconut oil or low-cal fry spray in a saucepan with the cumin, coriander, mixed spice, cinnamon and turmeric and fry for 1 minute over a medium heat. Immediately add the rice and a good pinch of salt and stir to coat. Add the lentils and the measured water, then bring to the boil, cover, reduce the heat to its lowest setting and simmer gently for 10–12 minutes, or until the rice is cooked. Take off the heat and uncover to allow any excess moisture to evaporate. Divide between 4 bowls and top each bowl with the sweet onions, yogurt, herbs and a squeeze of lemon to serve.

FAT (g): 23
PROTEIN (g): 41.7
CARBS (g): 14.7
FIBRE (g): 9.2
CALORIES: 451
SERVES: 2

Low in carb and lower in fat than the traditional recipe with no skimping on flavour, this featured on the show as part of a low-carb eating plan – which I hope you have gathered from this book, I'm a big fan of occasionally. Here, I've paired it with some grilled veggies to pack fibre and volume into the dish while keeping the calories moderate. Make sure you buy plain Greek yogurt and not Greek-style or flavoured, which can be loaded with added sugar. Natural yogurt is also good here.

REINVENTED TANDOORI CHICKEN BBQ

For the tandoor chicken, place the yogurt in a large bowl, add the garlic, ginger, lemon, tomato purée, spices and a good pinch of salt and pepper and stir together. Add the chicken and toss in the marinade. Cover with clingfilm and leave in the fridge for at least 1 hour or overnight.

When ready to cook, preheat the oven to 200°C/gas mark 6 and line a baking tray with foil.

Remove the chicken from the marinade and thread onto 2–4 metal skewers, discarding the marinade. Place the skewers on the prepared tray and bake in the oven for 25 minutes until cooked through and starting to crisp.

Meanwhile, for the salad, steam the beans to your liking and par-cook the broccoli for 2 minutes in a pan of boiling water. Drain and pat dry.

Heat a griddle pan over a high heat until hot. Lightly spritz the broccoli and courgette with low-cal fry spray and cook them in batches on the griddle pan

For the tandoor chicken

100g Greek or natural yogurt
1 garlic clove, crushed
5cm piece of fresh root ginger, grated,
    or 1 tsp fresh ginger paste
juice of 1 lemon
25g tomato purée
1 tsp garam masala
1 tsp ground coriander
1 tsp sweet smoked paprika
1 tsp chilli powder or cayenne pepper
1 tsp ground turmeric
salt and pepper
200g skinless chicken breast fillets, cut into
    2cm cubes

For the salad

100g green beans, trimmed
150g broccoli, cut into florets
1 courgette, thickly sliced
low-cal fry spray, for frying
2 large handfuls of baby spinach
40g walnuts, lightly toasted
juice of 1 lemon
1 tbsp extra virgin olive oil
salt and pepper

For the raita

100g Greek or natural yogurt
½ cucumber, coarsely grated
juice of 1 lemon
1 small bunch of mint or coriander or both,
    finely chopped
½ tsp garam masala
salt and pepper

until golden with char marks. Once cooked, tip into a bowl with the steamed beans and the spinach (chopped if raw spinach isn't your vibe) and walnuts. Dress the warm salad with the lemon juice, olive oil and a good pinch of salt and pepper.

For the raita, simply stir all the ingredients together with salt and pepper to taste in a bowl and set aside. This can be made in advance – just store it in the fridge until needed.

When ready to serve, pile up the charred veggies on a serving plate, top with the tandoori chicken (I like to leave it on the skewer for effect) and spoon over the raita. Serve with a lemon wedge and pickled red onions if you have any in the back of the fridge from the Christmas hamper.

FAT (g): 5
PROTEIN (g): 8.1
CARBS (g): 70.6
FIBRE (g): 3.6
CALORIES: 367
SERVES: 2

An instant crowd-pleaser, this risotto is ideal for a weekday dinner rather than a weekend lunch, as it's very quick to prepare. It's my version of a classic risotto, packed full of hidden veggies and not as labour intensive as a traditional risotto.

BAKED QUICK CREAMY RISOTTO

100g baby spinach
1 onion, finely chopped
1 celery stick, very finely chopped
1 garlic clove, finely chopped
2 tsp olive oil or low-cal fry spray
50ml white wine
150g arborio risotto rice
350ml hot vegetable stock
salt and pepper
150g mixed cherry tomatoes
2 tbsp mascarpone cheese (optional but tasty)
1 small bunch of basil, to serve

Throw the spinach into a large pan with a splash of water and steam for a minute or so until wilted. Drain on kitchen paper and roughly chop. Reserve.

Preheat the oven to 200°C/gas mark 6.

In an ovenproof pan or flameproof casserole dish, sauté the onion, celery and garlic in 1 tsp oil or low-cal fry spray over a low heat for about 8 minutes until softened. Increase the heat, add the wine and, once it is bubbling and has reduced a little stir in the rice, then immediately pour in the hot stock. Season well with salt and pepper, then cover with a lid and pop into the oven for 15 minutes. After 5 minutes, arrange the tomatoes in a roasting tray, drizzle with 1 tsp olive oil, season with salt and pepper and roast for the final 10 minutes.

Remove the risotto from the oven. Leave the tomatoes in but turn the oven off (the tomatoes will continue to cook in the heat of the oven). Stir the mascarpone, if using, and reserved chopped spinach into the risotto, then scatter the basil leaves over the top.

Serve the risotto with the sticky flavourful tomatoes either on the top or on the side. My lean protein of choice for this would be crispy roast chicken.

FAT (g): 35.8
PROTEIN (g): 48.9
CARBS (g): 6.6
FIBRE (g): 3.8
CALORIES: 552
SERVES: 2

This is a nourishing, comforting dish. Make sure you add a squeeze of lemon juice before serving, as vitamin C boosts the body's ability to absorb the plant-based iron in spinach. I've put oat bran in the crust as it's high in fibre and creates a feeling of fullness. The mornay is a lighter version of the classic; we've already skimped on the cream, saving 100 calories, so don't skimp on the milk – use whole not skimmed. Double up on the crumb mix and freeze for a speedy supper another time.

BAKED COD WITH A PINE NUT CRUST & SPINACH MORNAY

60g pine nuts
50g oat bran
1 handful of parsley, finely chopped
finely grated zest of 1 lemon
salt and pepper
1 egg
2 x 150g cod fillets or similar, skin removed

For the spinach mornay
1 tsp olive oil or 5g butter
1 shallot, finely chopped
1 garlic clove, finely chopped or grated
100g spinach
50ml whole milk
pinch of grated nutmeg
salt and pepper
80g lighter mature Cheddar cheese, grated

Preheat the oven to 220°C/gas mark 7.

For the spinach mornay, melt the oil or butter in a large frying pan over a low heat and fry the shallot and garlic for a few minutes until softened. Add the spinach and a few tbsp water, cover with a lid and steam for a minute or 2. Tip the spinach mixture out onto kitchen paper, pat dry, then roughly chop.

Arrange the spinach mixture in the base of a small ovenproof dish or 2 ramekins. Add the milk, nutmeg, some salt and pepper and stir, then scatter the cheese over the top. These can be made in advance and chilled for 24 hours until ready to use or frozen for 1 month tightly wrapped in clingfilm.

For the fish, roughly chop the pine nuts, place in a shallow dish, then add the bran, parsley, lemon zest and some salt and pepper and mix well. Beat the egg in a bowl. Lightly season the fish fillets, then dip the fillets into the egg and roll into the bran mix until coated. Place the coated fish on a baking tray and bake in the oven for 12–15 minutes until the fish is opaque and the crumbs golden. Pop the spinach mornay in at the same time on a lower shelf. If it begins to brown too quickly cover with a little foil.

Serve with steamed greens or a large leafy salad.

FAT (g): 14.1
PROTEIN (g): 53.8
CARBS (g): 21
FIBRE (g): 7.5
CALORIES: 441
SERVES: 2

Hands down the most requested recipe in the TV show's history, chicken tikka is traditionally made with around 6 teaspoons sugar; this one contains zero. The list of ingredients seems lengthy but the majority can be found in your storecupboard and there's nothing too fancy.

CHICKEN TIKKA MASALA

For the tikka
4 large chicken thighs, boned, skinned and cut into chunks (around 400g total)
salt and pepper
finely grated zest and juice of 1 lemon
1cm piece of fresh root ginger, peeled and grated
2 garlic cloves, crushed or grated
1 tsp ground cumin
1 tsp paprika
pinch of dried red chilli flakes, or to taste
1 tsp garam masala
6 tbsp full-fat natural yogurt

For the masala
2 tsp olive oil
1 onion, finely diced
2 garlic cloves, crushed
1cm piece of fresh root ginger, peeled and grated
1 tsp dried red chilli flakes, or to taste
1 bunch of coriander, leaves finely chopped
1 tsp ground turmeric
1 tbsp ground coriander
2 tsp paprika
2 beef tomatoes, deseeded and chopped into dice
200ml chicken stock
100ml full-fat natural yogurt
salt and pepper

Combine all the tikka ingredients together in a large bowl and massage the chicken thoroughly in the mixture. Cover with clingfilm and leave in the fridge for 30 minutes, or preferably overnight.

For the masala, heat the olive oil in a frying pan over a medium heat and sauté the onion, garlic, ginger and chilli flakes for 8 minutes. Add the coriander and spices and fry for a minute or so until fragrant. Add the tomatoes, stock and yogurt, then season with salt and pepper and simmer for 20 minutes.

When you're ready to eat, preheat the grill to its highest setting. Remove the chicken from the marinade, discarding the marinade, and either thread the chicken onto metal skewers or lay the chunks across the oven rack bars. Grill for about 5 minutes on each side or until cooked through and charred. This can also be done on a griddle pan, if you like.

Remove the chicken from the skewers, if using, stir through the masala sauce and serve immediately.

FAT (g): 36.1
PROTEIN (g): 11.6
CARBS (g): 25.7
FIBRE (g): 12.5
CALORIES: 499
SERVES: 2

This dish is based on the principles of the Ayurvedic diet where each meal should contain all six flavours: sweet, sour, salty, bitter, astringent and pungent. I love this as a side for an alternative Sunday lunch with some Mediterranean roast lamb. Roasting squash whole like this makes the skin easier to eat and deliciously sticky and sweet, which is a bonus considering it contains most of the nutrients.

ROAST SQUASH WITH FLAX PESTO

1 butternut squash, halved and deseeded
1 tsp olive oil
salt and pepper
sprinkle of dried red chilli flakes (optional but tasty)

For the flax pesto
1 small bunch of basil
1 small bunch of coriander or parsley
1 garlic clove
4 tbsp golden flaxseeds (linseeds)
25g grated Parmesan cheese (or nutritional yeast for slightly lower fat and fewer calories)
4 tbsp extra virgin olive oil
4 tbsp water
juice of 1 lemon
salt and pepper

Preheat the oven to 200°C/gas mark 6.

Score the squash all over with a sharp knife, then rub the olive oil all over and sprinkle with salt, pepper and chilli, if using. Place on a baking tray and roast in the oven for 30 minutes, or until tender.

For the flax pesto, simply whizz all the ingredients together with salt and pepper to taste in a blender. It should be pouring consistency, so you may need to thin it out with water or more lemon juice if needed.

Serve the squash warm with the pesto drizzled over. Simple, quick and delicious.

FAT (g): 9.9
PROTEIN (g): 10.1
CARBS (g): 19.6
FIBRE (g): 11.3
CALORIES: 231
SERVES: 2

This is a beautiful light lunch, packed full of flavour. Traditionally, noodles are used, but the raw courgette adds a real meaty texture to the dish and the sauce is to die for. It is our most requested sauce at my Eat Naked café. As the dish is seriously low carb, it is ideal for those days when you're not hitting the gym and are working on a lower-calorie base for the day.

MY PAD THAI WITH PEANUT SAUCE

"Bulk this out with some shredded leftover roast chicken, if you like."

For the salad
1 carrot, julienned, sliced or spiralized
1 courgette, julienned or spiralized
½ white cabbage, thinly sliced
100g sugar snap peas, sliced in half
2 handfuls of beansprouts
1 red pepper, thinly sliced
1 small bunch of coriander, roughly chopped
2 tsp sesame seeds, lightly toasted

For the peanut sauce
2 tsp toasted sesame oil
2 tsp soy sauce or tamari
2 tsp Thai Sriracha sauce or any low-sugar hot sauce
1 tbsp peanut butter
2 tbsp boiling water
juice of 1 lime

Toss all the salad ingredients together in a large bowl.

To make the peanut sauce, simply whisk everything together in a small bowl or put all the ingredients in a jam jar, cover with a lid and shake well.

The salad keeps for days in the fridge, as does the dressing, so mix them together when you're ready to serve.

FAT (g): 4.3
PROTEIN (g): 4.6
CARBS (g): 16.8
FIBRE (g): 4
CALORIES: 133
SERVES: 1

This is one of my go-to lunches as it's so versatile. Buddha bowls are very fashionable, but just think of them as kind of a deconstructed salad – a nourishing meal that's a little bite of everything. They encourage you to eat the rainbow and Instagram is brimming with the best ideas for presentation. I've given some ideas for how to build your bowl, but you can't go wrong with high-volume, low-cal veg. Just watch your portions on the healthy fats and beans – aim for 100g cooked beans or pulses, ½ avocado and 25g nuts. The nutritional info above is just for this one portion of falafel.

SESAME FALAFEL BUDDHA BOWL

2 medium carrots, roughly chopped
2 spring onions, roughly chopped
½ garlic clove
1 small bunch of coriander and/or parsley
1 tsp gluten-free baking powder
3 tbsp gluten-free flour
salt and pepper
1 tsp ground cumin
½ tsp smoked paprika
180g canned chickpeas, rinsed
a few tbsp sesame seeds, for coating
1 tsp coconut oil, for frying

Simply blitz all the ingredients, except the chickpeas, sesame seeds and coconut oil, in a food processor until smooth, then pulse in the chickpeas. If you like the mix smoother, blend the chickpeas fully.

Spread the sesame seeds out on a plate. Roll the mixture into 12 ping pong-sized balls and dip one side into the sesame seeds. Don't be tempted to roll the whole ball in, as that's double the calories.

Heat the oil in a frying pan over a high heat. When hot, turn down the heat to medium-high and fry the falafels for 2 minutes until the sesame seeds are golden, then flip over and roll around the pan to cook them on all sides. Fry for a further 3 minutes until golden and crispy. Remove from the pan and add 2 to your Buddha bowl. You can freeze or refrigerate the leftovers for another day.

BUILD A BUDDHA BOWL

Start with a base layer of greens: I love rocket and romaine, but any salad leaves are good.

Add a variety of veggies and beans: think grated carrot, edamame, courgette, diced avocado, red cabbage, cucumber, tomatoes, beetroot, sugar snap.

Add your complex carbs: such as brown rice, black beans, roast sweet potato, chickpeas, lentils or mung beans.

Add your nuts and seeds: you choose which ones, but stick to 25g.

Dress with your favourite sauce or dressing: make sure not to use too much oil and pimp up the flavours if you like with smoked paprika, harissa, herbs and a little lemon juice/oil/water combo to make a nice thick dressing.

To finish: your sesame falafels!

FAT (g): 24.7
PROTEIN (g): 8.1
CARBS (g): 10.7
FIBRE (g): 7.8
CALORIES: 313
SERVES: 2

A delicious, light fresh salad that doubles up as a cracking dinner with some grilled fish. Leafy greens are a great super-low-calorie, high-volume addition to your diet and offer countless health benefits. They are full of vitamins, minerals, and disease-fighting phytochemicals. Marinating the kale takes just minutes but it is essential for breaking down the tough leaves, so don't be tempted to skip this step. You can marinate the kale in advance; I do it in bulk, marinating whole bags at a time in the same dressing for different salads. It keeps for a few days in the fridge, no problem. If you have the fat macros, some goat's cheese crumbled over this is heaven.

FENNEL, BEAN, KALE & ORANGE SALAD WITH HAZELNUTS

"Adding 100g cooked grains to this salad is a good way to bulk it out while keeping it vegan."

2 tbsp extra virgin olive oil
1 orange, zest finely grated and then segmented
salt and pepper
1 tbsp apple cider vinegar
2 handfuls of kale, stalks removed and leaves chopped
100g green beans, trimmed
4 handfuls of rocket or leaves of choice
½ fennel bulb, thinly sliced (mandolin or attachment on a food processor is ideal)
40g hazelnuts, lightly toasted then roughly chopped

First, marinate the kale – then this is a throw-together spectacular! Combine the olive oil, orange zest, some salt and pepper, and the vinegar in a large bowl, throw in the kale and scrunch with your hands as if you are massaging it. Do this for a couple of minutes. Set aside.

Steam the beans for 3 minutes, or to your liking, then drain and plunge into a bowl of cold water to retain the green colour.

Throw the rocket in with the kale, followed by the drained green beans, the orange (and any juice that's escaped), and the fennel. Lightly toss together with your hands and if the salad needs a little more salt and pepper, go ahead. Finish with the hazelnuts.

FAT (g): 29.8
PROTEIN (g): 16.8
CARBS (g): 27.9
FIBRE (g): 7.9
CALORIES: 462
SERVES: 4

This is a bestseller at my café. We make it with around 2kg mung beans and it's gone within 45 minutes every time. It's delicious hot or cold, so adapt it to the seasons or how you're feeling. Mung beans are a great source of nutrients including manganese, potassium, magnesium, folate, copper, zinc and various B vitamins. They are super filling and high in protein and fibre, too.

COCONUT MUNG BEAN DAAL

150g dried mung beans
1 large white onion, finely sliced
1 garlic clove, finely sliced
5cm piece of fresh root ginger, peeled and grated
1 lemongrass stalk, outer leaves removed, roughly chopped, or 1 tsp fresh lemongrass paste
1 tsp coconut oil or low-cal fry spray
1 tsp ground turmeric
1 tsp garam masala
1 tsp ground cumin
1 tsp ground coriander
1 tsp mustard seeds (optional)
400ml can reduced-fat coconut milk
200ml vegetable stock or water
100g desiccated coconut
salt and pepper
dried red chilli flakes, to taste
1 small bunch of coriander, leaves chopped
40g peanuts, crushed
1 lime

Rinse the mung beans (don't worry – there's no need to pre-soak them).

Place the onion, garlic, ginger and lemongrass in a mini chopper and blend until fine. You can do this by hand if you are using fresh lemongrass paste.

Heat the oil in a large saucepan over a medium heat and sauté the onion mix for 8 minutes until soft. Increase the heat and immediately add the spices and mustard seeds, if using. Stir for a minute or so until fragrant, being careful not to let the spices burn. Add the coconut milk, stock, desiccated coconut and the drained mung beans. Season with salt and pepper and add dried chilli flakes to taste. Bring to the boil briefly, then reduce the heat and simmer for 40 minutes.

Serve hot or cold topped with coriander and crushed peanuts, and lime wedges to squeeze over. Once cold the daal will thicken up, but is easily broken up with a fork.

FAT (g): 20.7
PROTEIN (g): 10.1
CARBS (g): 22
FIBRE (g): 13.3
CALORIES: 341
SERVES: 2

This high-protein, high-vitamin, high-fibre combination is a great make-ahead dish. I pair this with chunky tiger prawns or shredded roast chicken, but it's fantastic on its own as the mushrooms add a delicious meaty texture and pack in the B vitamins, as well as vitamin D. As a little bonus health tip, I enjoy scrunching up a pack of wasabi-flavoured dried seaweed sheets over the top of this salad for a super-low calorie crunch.

SESAME KALE SALAD

4 handfuls of kale, stalks removed and leaves roughly torn or chopped
100g shiitake mushrooms, cut into thin slices
2 medium carrots, julienned, spiralized or coarsely grated
1 cucumber, julienned, spiralized or coarsely grated
½ white or red cabbage, sliced as thinly as possible
2 tbsp sesame seeds, lightly toasted
1 small bunch of coriander or mint, or a mix of both, chopped

For the dressing
1 tbsp extra virgin olive oil
juice of 1 orange
2 tbsp soy sauce or tamari
1 tbsp sesame oil
salt and pepper

Mix all the dressing ingredients together in a large bowl, then tumble the kale on top. Using your hands, massage the kale with the dressing. Add the mushrooms and toss well. Cover with clingfilm and leave to marinate in the fridge. You can marinate the kale and mushrooms the night before or even a few days in advance, if you like.

When ready to serve, add the carrots, cucumber, cabbage, seeds and herbs to the bowl and toss everything together.

FAT (g): 19.9
PROTEIN (g): 23.6
CARBS (g): 55.5
FIBRE (g): 18.9
CALORIES: 533
SERVES: 2

This is a super-sneaky way of packing in the veggies and they don't even have to be cooked, meaning not only is this salad really quick, it's also very nutritious since the veg retain 100 per cent of their nutrients. This is my go-to salad after the gym. It's packed with slow-release carbs, fibre and plant-based protein as well as healthy fats from the nuts. I've used kidney beans here, as they contain more antioxidants and omega-3 fatty acids than any other beans, as well as being high in thiamine which helps the body to release energy from food. A gym goer's delight.

POST-GYM SUPER WHOLEFOOD NUTTY SALAD

"This is my ultimate container salad, perfect on a picnic, too, as the dressing can be tossed through in advance."

100g quinoa
1 head of broccoli, blitzed or chopped into small chunks
100g green beans, trimmed and chopped
1 large carrot, grated
200g canned kidney beans, drained and rinsed
4 tbsp nuts of choice, lightly toasted then roughly chopped
1 small bunch of herbs of choice (I love coriander with this)
salt and pepper

For the dressing
5cm piece of fresh root ginger, peeled and grated
2 tbsp soy sauce or tamari
1 tbsp extra virgin olive oil
1 tbsp water
salt and pepper
1 tsp honey or maple syrup

Place the quinoa in a pan, cover with boiling water, bring to the boil briefly, cover with a lid and steam for 12 minutes. All of the water should have been absorbed in this time – if it hasn't, turn the heat off, uncover and allow any excess moisture to evaporate. Alternatively, cook the quinoa according to the packet instructions.

Whisk all the dressing ingredients together in a small bowl, then dress the quinoa while it's still warm to infuse all the flavours.

Allow the quinoa to cool, then toss the rest of the veggies, beans, nuts and herbs through the quinoa and mix thoroughly. Season with salt and pepper, to taste, if needed, and enjoy.

FAT (g): 12.5
PROTEIN (g): 24.8
CARBS (g): 57.1
FIBRE (g): 16.2
CALORIES: 473
SERVES: 2

Here is a comforting dish full of complex spices that keeps for days and gets better as it ages. Black lentils are sometimes called beluga lentils; they are tiny and pretty and stay perfectly intact when you cook them. If you have green lentils in your storecupboard, they work just as well here.

SPICED BLACK DAAL WITH COCONUT YOGURT

150g black lentils
1 onion, roughly chopped
1 garlic clove, roughly chopped
5cm piece of fresh root ginger, peeled
1 tsp coconut oil
1 cinnamon stick
4 cloves
1 tsp fennel seeds
2 star anise
1 tsp ground turmeric
1 tsp garam masala
1 tsp ground cumin
1 tsp ground coriander
200ml stock of choice
140g tube of tomato purée
salt and pepper
½ tsp dried red chilli flakes, or to taste
2 tbsp unsweetened coconut (or natural) yogurt
a few coriander leaves
1 tbsp sesame seeds, lightly toasted

Rinse the black lentils and leave to drain.

Blend the onion, garlic and ginger in a mini chopper.

Heat the coconut oil in a large saucepan and cook the onion mixture for 8 minutes until soft.

Meanwhile, fry the cinnamon, cloves, fennel seeds and star anise in a dry pan over a medium-low heat for a few minutes until fragrant. Transfer to a mortar and crush with the pestle until fine. Alternatively, use a coffee or spice grinder or buy ready ground spices. Transfer to a small bowl, add the rest of the spices and toss together.

Increase the heat under the onions and throw in all the spices. Fry over a medium-high heat for a minute, stirring constantly to make sure the spices don't burn. Pour in the stock, then add the tomato purée, some salt and pepper, the chilli flakes and the drained lentils. Bring to the boil briefly, then reduce the heat and simmer for 30 minutes, or until the lentils are tender. Add more liquid if the pan begins to dry or you prefer a wetter daal.

When ready to serve, divide the daal between 2 bowls and top with the yogurt, coriander and sesame seeds.

FAT (g): 27.4
PROTEIN (g): 47.7
CARBS (g): 9.7
FIBRE (g): 5.5
CALORIES: 487
SERVES: 2

This ultra-low-carb, lean burger doesn't need the bun, but if you insist on an edible 'handle', try wrapping it in iceberg leaves with thick slices of tomato and pickles.

TURKEY FETA BURGERS WITH CORN & CHILLI LIME BUTTER

1 tsp olive oil or low-cal fry spray
½ small red onion, very finely chopped
1 garlic clove, grated, chopped or minced
100g baby spinach
100g feta cheese, crumbled
300g turkey mince
1 egg yolk
salt and pepper
1 tsp dried oregano
dried red chilli flakes (optional)

For the corn & chilli lime butter
10g butter
dried red chilli flakes, to taste
finely grated zest of 1 lime
½ tsp ground cumin
a few sprigs of coriander leaves, very finely chopped
2 mini corn-on-the-cobs

Heat the olive oil or low-cal fry spray in a frying pan over a medium heat and fry the onion for 1 minute until starting to soften, then add the garlic and fry for a few seconds. Add the spinach, reduce the heat to low, cover the pan (a plate is fine) and cook for a minute or so until the spinach has wilted. Drain the spinach, onion and garlic mix on kitchen paper, then roughly chop or blend in a mini chopper.

In a large bowl, add the chopped spinach mixture, the feta, turkey mince, egg yolk, some salt and pepper and oregano (a little chilli is nice here, too, if you fancy) and mix everything together until all the ingredients are evenly distributed. Form into 4 patties that are at least 2cm thick, then place the patties on a lined tray and allow to rest in the fridge or freezer for about 10 minutes. This can be done in advance.

Very lightly oil a non-stick frying pan just so the burgers don't stick, then heat over a medium heat. When hot, cook the burgers for 6 minutes on each side. Leave them alone during this time, otherwise they may break up. Make sure the burgers are cooked thoroughly before removing them from the pan.

Meanwhile, for the corn, heat the butter, chilli flakes to taste, lime zest and ground cumin gently in a small saucepan until the butter has melted. Take off the heat and add the coriander. This can be done in advance. Transfer to a small ramekin and keep in the fridge until needed.

Simply steam the corn for about 6 minutes until tender, then spoon over the butter or, if you've left it to chill, allow to melt over the warm cob.

SEPARATE NUTRITIONAL BREAKDOWN FOR CORN & CHILLI LIME BUTTER ALONE

Fat 5.7g; protein 3g; carbs 7.3g, fibre 4.3g; calories 101

FAT (g): 36.2
PROTEIN (g): 37.7
CARBS (g): 11.5
FIBRE (g): 2
CALORIES: 527
SERVES: 2

This is a wonderful summer dish which takes about 20 minutes from start to finish. You can use an indoor grill or barbecue for the fish, making this a versatile recipe that's naturally low in calories and high in protein. Substitute the potatoes for a big leafy salad if you're on the Kickstart plan. This is a great high-volume meal for a fasting day, too. The salsa verde can be made in advance and kept in an airtight container in the fridge to dress a variety of dishes through the book.

GRILLED FISH, SALSA VERDE & POTATOES

150g new potatoes, unpeeled
salt and pepper
5g butter
1 tbsp finely chopped chives (optional)
2 x 200g white fish fillets with the skin on, such as sea bass, cod or halibut, skin scored lightly
1 tsp olive oil, for brushing
1 lemon, halved

For the salsa verde
3 handfuls of herbs (a mix of tarragon, parsley, mint, dill and coriander)
½ garlic clove
1 tbsp capers
salt and pepper
½ tsp Dijon mustard (optional)
1 tbsp cornichons (optional)
2 anchovy fillets (optional)
4 tbsp extra virgin olive oil
2 tbsp water
juice of 1 lemon

Steam the potatoes until tender, then crush with a fork, season with a little salt and pepper, add the butter and throw in the chives, if using.

Meanwhile, make the salsa verde. The quick way is to throw it all in a mini chopper or blender and blend until smooth. Alternatively, very finely chop everything by hand and stir in the oil, water and lemon juice to make a thick emerald slushy sauce. Taste and add a little more lemon, if you like.

When you're ready to cook the fish, preheat the grill to its highest setting. Brush the skin lightly with oil and season the fillets all over with salt and pepper. Cut one lemon half into slices and lay the fish skin side up on top of the slices, in a roasting tray. Grill for 4 minutes until the skin is crisp, then flip over and grill for 1 minute skin side down, or until cooked through, opaque and just starting to flake apart. Serve with the second lemon half to squeeze over the fish, alongside the salsa verde and potatoes.

FAT (g): 25.3
PROTEIN (g): 40
CARBS (g): 14.7
FIBRE (g): 9.1
CALORIES: 464
SERVES: 2

This is another flavour-packed, high-volume, low-calorie meal that I enjoy on fasting days. There's no fuss to this dish – it's prepared in under 15 minutes and loaded with super-healthy omega-3 fatty acids. Pick and choose your veggies based on what you like, but remember they are high-volume foods so you can't really go wrong with loading up.

THAI POACHED SALMON BOWL

2 shallots, chopped
1 thumb-sized piece of fresh root ginger, peeled and chopped
2 garlic cloves, chopped
1 red chilli, deseeded and chopped
1 lemongrass stalk, outer leaves removed, chopped, or 1 tbsp fresh lemongrass paste
1 tsp coconut oil
400ml fish, chicken or vegetable stock
2 salmon fillets (about 140g each), skin removed
1 bunch of pak choi (about 6 leaves)
150g beansprouts
1 carrot, julienned or very thinly sliced
1 red pepper, thinly sliced
1 courgette, julienned
1 tbsp fish sauce (optional)
1 lime
1 tsp sesame seeds, lightly toasted
1 small bunch of coriander, Thai basil and/or mint, roughly chopped

In a mini chopper, whizz the shallots, ginger, garlic, chilli and lemongrass (if using lemongrass paste, don't add that at this stage) until you have a paste.

Heat the oil in a medium-large saucepan over a medium-low heat and fry the shallot paste for a few minutes to soften. Pour in the stock and bring to a simmer. Add the lemongrass paste now, if using. Simmer for 10 minutes to infuse the flavours. If you're in a rush this isn't necessary.

When you're ready to poach the salmon, simply add the fillets to the hot stock and simmer gently for 6–8 minutes. For the last 2 minutes, add the pak choi and beansprouts.

Meanwhile, arrange the carrot, red pepper and courgette in a pile in the middle of 2 serving bowls. Place the poached fish on top, then add the fish sauce to the stock, if using, before ladling the fragrant stock mixture over the dish. Add a squeeze of lime juice before serving and top with the sesame seeds and herbs.

NOTE

If you don't like the veg as crunchy, add them to the stock for the last minute to soften a little.

FAT (g): 14.4
PROTEIN (g): 17.5
CARBS (g): 47.9
FIBRE (g): 12.3
CALORIES: 416
SERVES: 2

This is probably one of the best veggie mains I make. It flies out as a special every week in my café, as it's fresh, healthy and delicious with lots of textures. This dish is great as a side at a barbecue, too. Pair it with a large green salad for lunch or have it as an accompaniment for dinner. It goes amazingly well with Monday's Crispy Lamb on page 84.

ROAST SQUASH, CARDAMOM & LIME YOGURT, POMEGRANATE & SPICY SEED GRANOLA

1 butternut squash, deseeded and cut into 8 long fingers (quarter then halve the quarters)
1 tsp ground allspice
1 tsp olive oil
salt and pepper
seeds of 1 small pomegranate
1 small bunch of coriander, mint and/or parsley

For the yogurt
4 tbsp Greek, natural live or coconut yogurt
½ tsp fresh lemongrass paste
½ tsp ground cardamom
finely grated zest of 1 lime

For the spicy seed granola
50g mixed seeds
2 tsp honey
pinch of dried red chilli flakes
salt and pepper

Preheat the oven to 220°C/gas mark 7 and line a baking tray with baking paper.

Lay the squash on the prepared baking tray, skin side down.

In a small bowl, combine the allspice, oil and some salt and pepper. Brush or drizzle this mix over the squash, making sure the pieces are evenly coated. Roast the squash in the oven for 30 minutes, or until burnished, golden and tender. The skin should be sticky sweet.

For the yogurt, simply stir all the ingredients together in a bowl and reserve.

Toast the mixed seeds in a hot, dry pan over medium heat until they begin to crackle. Take off the heat and add the honey, chilli flakes, salt and pepper. Swirl the pan to coat the seeds, then tip out onto a piece of baking paper and allow to cool.

Once the seeds are cooled, break them apart and scatter them over the finished dish with the pomegranate seeds, herbs and juice of the lime that was zested earlier.

FAT (g): 19.9
PROTEIN (g): 49.2
CARBS (g): 25.2
FIBRE (g): 6.9
CALORIES: 490
SERVES: 2

It's worth roasting the chicken for this. It's cheaper than buying individual cuts, and you can make better use of cuts like the thighs, which are more cheaper than breast meat. Lighten the load even more by having this as Monday's lunch after a Sunday roast. Chicken aside, this recipe requires no other cooking. The zesty flavours are delicious for few calories, and there's lots of volume to fill you up. The dipping sauce is a great fridge staple so I've given a larger yield for a few different uses, but stick to 2 tbsp as a portion.

SESAME CHICKEN SALAD WITH CUCUMBER NOODLES & SWEET CHILLI DIPPING SAUCE

1 cucumber, julienned or spiralized
½ head of Chinese cabbage, finely sliced, or 100g your favourite salad leaves
4 spring onions, finely sliced
150g beansprouts
1 small bunch of coriander, mint and Thai basil, chopped
1 red chilli, very finely sliced (deseeded if you prefer)
1 head of pak choi, stems halved lengthways, raw or steamed for 1 minute
300g roast chicken, shredded
1 tsp sesame seeds, lightly toasted

For the sweet chilli dipping sauce
75ml maple syrup
50ml apple cider vinegar
1 tbsp dried red chilli flakes or 1 red chilli, finely chopped
1 tsp cornflour
salt and pepper
2 garlic cloves, crushed
100ml water

For the dressing
1 tbsp toasted sesame oil
finely grated zest and juice of 1 lime
1 tsp honey
1 tbsp tamari or soy sauce
1 tsp tamarind paste (optional)

For the sweet chilli dipping sauce, place all the ingredients in a saucepan, bring to the boil, then reduce the heat and simmer for a few minutes until thickened. Allow to cool, then store in the fridge.

Place the cucumber in a large bowl, add the cabbage or salad leaves, spring onions, beansprouts, herbs, chilli and pak choi and toss to combine.

Whizz or whisk all the dressing ingredients together, then pour into a bowl, add the roast chicken and mix together. Toss the chicken through the salad with any extra dressing, a sprinkle of the sesame seeds and we are done! How quick was that?

FAT (g): 7.4
PROTEIN (g): 24.1
CARBS (g): 36.1
FIBRE (g): 9.8
CALORIES: 327
SERVES: 2

This flavour-packed salad is high volume and low calorie, meaning you can munch through the veggies to your heart's content and it'll fill you up in a flash. Nam jim is a traditional Thai dressing and is hot, sour and tangy. If you're on the Kickstart plan, substitute the noodles for courgetti or cucumber noodles.

FLASH PRAWNS IN A JAR WITH CRUNCHY SALAD & NAM JIM

12 large raw king or tiger prawns, shelled and deveined
salt and pepper
1 tsp coconut oil, for frying
1 small red chilli, deseeded (optional) and finely chopped
2cm piece of fresh root ginger, peeled and finely chopped
1 garlic clove, finely chopped

For the nam jim
2 tbsp fish sauce
finely grated zest and juice of 1 lime
1 small garlic clove
2.5cm piece of fresh root ginger, peeled
½ small red onion or 2 shallots
3 red bird's eye chillies, or to taste
1 small bunch of coriander
2 tbsp tamari or soy sauce
1 tbsp toasted sesame oil
1 tsp coconut sugar or honey (optional)

For the salad
1 sheet of medium egg noodles, or try kelp noodles
1 carrot, julienned
½ small white cabbage, finely shredded
1 small handful of sugar snap peas
1 small handful of beansprouts
1 tsp toasted sesame oil (optional)

To serve
lime wedges
2 tsp sesame seeds, lightly toasted

For the nam jim, either finely chop all the ingredients together and mix in the liquid ingredients or blend everything in a blender until smooth. You will only need 4 tbsp in this dish, so keep the rest in a jam jar in the fridge.

For the salad, cook the egg noodles according to the packet instructions.

Place the carrot and cabbage in a large bowl with the sugar snaps, beansprouts and cooked, drained noodles. Toss everything together – you may need to add the sesame oil to loosen the noodles as they can stick.

Lightly season the prawns with salt and pepper. Heat a frying pan or wok until hot over a high heat, add the oil, then the chilli, ginger and garlic and stir-fry briskly for 30 seconds. Add the prawns and stir-fry for about 2 minutes, or until they turn a beautiful coral pink.

Divide one-quarter of the salad between 2 jars, top with 3 prawns and 1 tbsp of the nam jim, then repeat this layering process one more time. Add a lime wedge and a sprinkle of sesame seeds to the top of the jar before sealing and popping in the fridge ready.

FAT (g): 55.6
PROTEIN (g): 40.1
CARBS (g): 58.3
FIBRE (g): 22.8
CALORIES: 940
SERVES: 2

A hearty, healthy salad with punchy flavours and meaty textures. Lentils contain protein and high levels of soluble fibre, making this a great work lunch to help you fight off afternoon hunger pangs. The red cabbage and beetroot add volume while keeping the calories low, as well as containing antioxidants and vitamins. The nuts, seeds and cheese add healthy fats – specifically the walnuts, which are an excellent source of anti-inflammatory omega-3 fatty acids.

PUY LENTILS, PICKLED RED CABBAGE & BEETROOT SALAD WITH FETA & WALNUTS

"Speed-up tip: use good-quality precooked lentils to make this dish in under 10 minutes."

150g Puy lentils
½ red cabbage, sliced as thinly as possible (a mandolin is good for this)
4 tbsp red wine vinegar
4 tbsp extra virgin olive oil
1 tbsp tamari (optional)
salt and pepper
250g cooked beetroot, drained and chopped (not the jarred beetroot in vinegar)
a few handfuls of herbs, such as parsley, coriander and mint, finely chopped
finely grated zest and juice of 1 lemon
seeds of 1 small pomegranate
100g feta cheese, crumbled
20g walnuts, lightly toasted
4 tbsp pumpkin seeds, lightly toasted

Rinse the lentils and cook according to the packet instructions. Two minutes before the end of cooking, uncover and allow the lentils to steam to get rid of any excess moisture. Remove from the heat and allow the lentils to cool slightly.

Place the cabbage in a bowl, add the vinegar, oil and tamari, if using, with a good pinch of salt, and toss and scrunch the cabbage into the dressing. Reserve.

Once the lentils have cooled a little, add the cabbage, beetroot, herbs, lemon zest and juice, some salt and pepper and the pomegranate seeds, then toss the feta through gently so it doesn't break up too much. Divide between 2 bowls and top with the nuts and pumpkin seeds. If you have the calorie allowance for the day, finish with a glug of the finest extra virgin oil before serving.

FAT (g): 8.5
PROTEIN (g): 27.7
CARBS (g): 48.1
FIBRE (g): 3.7
CALORIES: 387
SERVES: 2

Crispy, low calorie and loaded with protein, these patties are good hot or cold and are an amazing side dish to pretty much any salad in this book. Courgette is a great high-volume, low-calorie food so I've used it here to bulk out the patties, giving you more for your calories – but spinach could also be used instead. The patties can be frozen, too; simply cook according to the instructions, freeze them wrapped in threes, defrost when you need them and reheat in a 190°C/gas mark 5 oven for 10 minutes (or microwave but they won't be crispy). These go well with the Spicy Avocado Dip on page 80 or the Sweet Chilli Dipping Sauce on page 116 and the Salsa Verde on page 110.

PRAWN, COURGETTE & QUINOA PATTIES

1 courgette
200g raw king prawns, shelled, deveined and roughly chopped
½ red onion, finely chopped
1 garlic clove, finely chopped
1 very small handful of parsley, finely chopped (use about 4 tsp)
80g cooked quinoa
pinch of dried red chilli flakes
90g flour of choice (not coconut – it doesn't work here)
2 eggs, lightly beaten
salt and pepper
coconut oil, for frying

Grate the courgette, then place it on a sheet of kitchen paper and wring out the excess water. Place the courgette in a large bowl with the remaining ingredients, except the coconut oil. Season well with salt and pepper and mix thoroughly.

Using your hands, form the mixture into 6 patties. You can leave them to chill in the fridge or cook them straightaway.

When ready to cook, heat the coconut oil in a large frying pan over a medium-high heat, and when hot, carefully add the patties. Fry for 3–4 minutes on one side until golden and crisp, then flip and cook for a further 3–4 minutes. Serve warm or cold.

ENTERTAINING

Being on a diet doesn't have to mean your social life stops. One of my favourite pastimes is having friends round for dinner, chatting and eating and making memories. And I'm not interested in cooking separate meals for people. I firmly believe there is a one-size-fits-all for most meals and we can just tweak the sides. Here I've compiled a selection of my best showstoppers, dishes which in some instances take that little bit of extra time to prepare but look fantastic AND are still compatible with your macros. Which means you can still eat healthily and enjoy all aspects of a social life without feeling deprived or like you're missing out. Most of the recipes serve two, as each one makes a lovely evening meal for midweek, too.

FAT (g): 34.2
PROTEIN (g): 34.7
CARBS (g): 52.9
FIBRE (g): 21.6
CALORIES: 701
SERVES: 2

An instant hit on the TV show, this dish impressed everyone when I presented it on the Blood Sugar Diet, a diet which claims to help reset insulin levels and even reverse type-2 diabetes. Freekeh is a young green wheat that has been toasted and cracked. It's a healthy wholegrain food much like bulgur wheat, but meatier and nuttier. You can buy it in most major supermarkets.

MIDDLE EASTERN STUFFED AUBERGINE WITH FREEKEH PILAF

"If you prefer, you can buy the freekeh dried and cook it yourself, but using the precooked variety saves you lots of time."

2 aubergines, halved lengthways
2 tsp olive oil
salt and pepper
1 onion, finely chopped
½ garlic clove, finely chopped
1 tsp ground cumin
1 tsp paprika
1 tsp ground cinnamon
150g lean lamb mince
2 tbsp tomato purée or 200g canned chopped tomatoes
100ml lamb, chicken or vegetable stock
1 small bunch of herbs, such as coriander, parsley and/or mint, finely chopped
seeds from 1 pomegranate
2 tbsp pine nuts, lightly toasted
yogurt, such as Greek, to serve

For the pilaf
1 tsp olive oil
1 onion, thinly sliced
½ garlic clove, finely chopped
½ tsp ground cinnamon
½ tsp ground allspice
150g ready-to-eat freekah
juice of 1 lemon
4 tbsp flaked almonds, lightly toasted
salt and pepper

Preheat the oven to 220°C/gas mark 7.

Make deep incisions in the aubergines, either slashes or a criss-cross three-quarters of the way through the flesh, then brush the aubergines with 1 tsp olive oil and season with salt and pepper. Place on a baking tray and roast in the oven for 30 minutes until golden and tender.

Meanwhile, heat the remaining 1 tsp olive oil in a medium saucepan, then fry the onion and garlic for about 8 minutes over a low-medium heat to soften. Increase the heat and throw in the cumin, paprika and cinnamon, stir briefly, then add the mince and season with salt and pepper. Stir well, then stir in the tomato purée or tomatoes and stock. Let bubble, then reduce the heat, cover with a lid and simmer for 20–40 minutes until the meat is lovely and tenderized. Five minutes before the end, uncover to let the juices evaporate. The meat mix should be quite dry not saucy.

For the pilaf, heat the oil in another pan, and sauté the onion and garlic for 8 minutes until softened. Increase the heat, add the cinnamon and allspice. Add the freekah, then reduce the heat to low and gently warm the freekah through for a minute or so. You can add a splash of water for a light steam if you like. Stir in the lemon juice, flaked almonds and salt and pepper. Keep warm until you're ready.

Spoon the pilaf between 2 serving plates, top with the aubergine, then divide the lamb mix between the 4 aubergine halves. Finish with a scattering of the herbs, pomegranate seeds, pine nuts and 1 tbsp each of Greek yogurt.

NUTRITIONAL BREAKDOWN FOR PILAF ALONE

Fat 13.1g; protein 8.8g; carbs 29.7g, fibre 8.6g; calories 289

FAT (g): 16.7
PROTEIN (g): 55.2
CARBS (g): 20
FIBRE (g): 7.8
CALORIES: 467
SERVES: 2

This contains lots of hidden veggies, contributing heavily to your 5-a-day. Serve to your guests with a mezze board and chunky bread for dipping. For yourself, savour and enjoy the flavours! If you're on the Shapeshifter or Transformer meal plans, feel free to add 100g canned cannellini beans to turn this into a hearty broth. A speed-up tip here is to use pre-cut chorizo. Most supermarkets sell it packaged and ready diced; it'll save you time skinning and chopping a whole chorizo, plus they are usually in 70g pouches. This is a low-carb, high-protein and high-fibre dish so it's great for Kickstarters and it's good on fasting days, too.

5-A-DAY SPANISH BRAISED CHICKEN & CHORIZO STEW

60g chorizo, diced
1 red onion, thinly sliced
1 garlic clove, finely chopped
1 tsp ground cumin
1 tsp dried oregano
1 tsp smoked paprika
400g boneless, skinless chicken thighs (about 4–5)
400g can chopped tomatoes
about 100ml water
salt and pepper
1 red pepper, chopped into chunks
1 tsp olive oil
2 small courgettes, chopped into chunks
1 bunch of flat leaf parsley, finely chopped,
    to garnish

Heat a large saucepan over a medium heat, add the chorizo and fry for a few minutes to release the tasty juices. There's no need to add extra oil here, as enough comes from the chorizo. Reduce the heat to low, add the onion and garlic and sauté for a few minutes, stirring to make sure the chorizo doesn't burn.

Add the cumin, oregano and paprika and stir until everything is coated. Increase the heat and add the chicken. Stir briefly, then add the tomatoes, water and salt and pepper. Cover with a lid, bring it to the boil briefly, then reduce the heat and simmer gently for 40 minutes, or until the chicken is super tender. Five minutes before the end of cooking, add the pepper.

Meanwhile, heat the oil in a separate pan over a medium heat, then sauté the courgette for 10 minutes until golden on all sides. Add the courgette to the chicken just before serving.

Divide the broth between 2 bowls and garnish with parsley.

FAT (g): 37.3
PROTEIN (g): 56.2
CARBS (g): 18
FIBRE (g): 3.4
CALORIES: 639
SERVES: 4

This is an unbelievably rich dish that's very cheap to make. The preparation is quick and easy – it's resisting eating it while it's cooking that's the hard part. This is a true throw-it-in-and-leave-it-for-hours dish, meaning you can focus on entertaining. The curry is thick and dry, so serve this with the spicy cauliflower rice on page 139 for yourself, and basmati for your guests. You don't need to buy palm sugar specifically – coconut or brown sugar work fine. I've specifically made this for four people, as it does take a little time and leftovers are always a bonus for a speedy lunch or dinner tomorrow. The mango chutney is an optional but tasty side. It makes plenty, so it can be kept in the fridge for other uses; just stick to 1 tbsp for a portion though.

THROW-IT-IN BEEF RENDANG & MANGO CHUTNEY

1kg brisket, cut into 4 pieces
3 tbsp good-quality Thai red curry paste
1 tbsp olive oil
2 shallots, finely chopped
2 garlic cloves, finely chopped
4 cardamom pods
2 star anise
2 cinnamon sticks, snapped in half
1 lemongrass stalk, bashed to release flavour
2 kaffir lime leaves (optional)
1 tbsp ground cumin
1 tbsp ground coriander
400ml can coconut milk
200ml beef stock
1 tsp salt and pepper

For the mango chutney
5cm piece of fresh root ginger, peeled and grated
2 garlic cloves, grated
100ml apple cider vinegar
3 tbsp coconut sugar, maple syrup or soft brown sugar
1 tsp black onion seeds (also known as nigella seeds),
    optional
½ cinnamon stick
1 tsp ground turmeric
1 tsp dried red chilli flakes
salt and pepper
1 apple, grated
1 ripe mango, peeled, stoned and diced into 1cm cubes

To finish
1 tbsp fish sauce
1 tsp caster sugar mixed with 1 tsp tamarind paste
juice of 1 lime

To serve
steamed basmati or spicy cauliflower rice
    (see page 139, but without the spices)
finely chopped coriander
lime wedges

Preheat the oven to 150°C/gas mark 2.

Put the meat in a bowl, cover it in the curry paste and cover the bowl with clingfilm. Marinate in the fridge for a few hours, or preferably overnight.

For the mango chutney, place the ginger, garlic, vinegar, sugar, spices and salt and pepper in a saucepan and bring to the boil. Add the apple and mango and simmer for 30 minutes, or until thickened. Allow to cool and keep in airtight container or a jam jar in the fridge for up to 2 weeks.

When you are ready to start cooking, heat the oil in a medium saucepan over a medium heat, then sauté the shallots and garlic for about 8 minutes until soft. Increase the heat, add the cardamom, star anise, cinnamon, lemongrass, lime leaves, ground cumin and ground coriander and stir the spices into the oil for a few seconds. Keep the heat high, add the marinated beef and quickly seal on all sides. Add the coconut milk and beef stock to just cover the meat and bring to the boil. Cover with a lid and cook in the oven for up to 4 hours; the longer you leave it the better, but it will be ready after 3 hours.

Uncover the pan 30–40 minutes before the end of the cooking time to allow the sauce to thicken. It will thicken further once the meat is shredded through the sauce. As soon as the brisket is cooked, shred the beef in the sauce with 2 forks. Stir in the finishing ingredients, being careful to balance the sweet, sour, salty and hot flavourings and serve with the steamed rice, coriander, lime wedges and mango chutney. Remove the cinnamon sticks, lemongrass, lime leaves and star anise before tucking in.

FAT (g): 43.5
PROTEIN (g): 59.1
CARBS (g): 33.7
FIBRE (g): 4.1
CALORIES: 771
SERVES: 4

Wow your friends and family with this unusual but flavour-packed beef dish using short ribs, which are inexpensive. After some initial prep, you just let the meat simmer before adding the tasty glaze. The result is delicious, saucy, fall-off-the-bone meat. This is perfect in a slow cooker, too.

VIETNAMESE SHORT RIBS & BROWN RICE

4 x beef short ribs
1 tsp five-spice powder
1 tsp dark brown sugar
salt and pepper
1 tsp olive oil
2 onions, finely diced
4 garlic cloves, finely chopped
5cm piece of fresh root ginger, peeled and finely chopped
2 star anise
300ml beef stock
100ml rice vinegar
160g steamed brown rice

To finish
4 tsp honey (optional)
2 tbsp Asian fish sauce
2 tbsp soy sauce or tamari
juice of 2 limes
1 medium bunch of coriander, finely chopped
4 tbsp peanuts, finely chopped
1 red chilli, finely sliced and deseeded if preferred

Preheat the oven to 150°C/gas mark 2 if you prefer to cook the ribs in the oven rather than on the hob.

Rub the ribs in the five-spice powder, sugar and salt and pepper and set aside.

Heat the oil in a large saucepan over a high heat, add the ribs and seal on all sides. Scoop the ribs out, reduce the heat to medium and add the onions, garlic, ginger and star anise. Sauté for about 8 minutes. Increase the heat again and add the stock and vinegar. When it's simmering, lower the heat to low, add the short ribs back to the pan, cover with a lid and simmer for 2–4 hours. They'll be done after 2 hours but they are even better after 4. Alternatively, transfer everything to a casserole dish, cover with a lid and bake for 2–4 hours. (Just as for the hob, they'll be done after 2 hours but they are even better after 4.)

Uncover, scoop out the ribs and bring the sauce to a rapid boil to reduce. At this point, rub the ribs with 1 tsp honey per rib and grill over a high heat to caramelize the meat, if you like.

When the sauce is as thick as you like it, turn the heat off and add the fish sauce, soy sauce and the lime juice.

Spoon the sauce over the ribs and top with coriander, peanuts and chilli. Serve with the steamed rice.

FAT (g): 17.6
PROTEIN (g): 53.6
CARBS (g): 19
FIBRE (g): 3.9
CALORIES: 456
SERVES: 2

Here's a dish no one will suspect came from a diet book. The courgette noodles add texture and volume with very few carbohydrates and calories. Loaded with healthy fats and protein, this is a perfect dish for entertaining as it's so low calorie you can afford to have a small portion of pudding, too, or a small glass of wine.

CASHEW CHICKEN WITH COURGETTI & CORIANDER

80ml tamari or soy sauce
1 tbsp cornflour or arrowroot
2 garlic cloves, grated
400g boneless, skinless chicken thighs (about 4–5)
1 tsp olive oil
4 spring onions, thinly sliced
40g cashew nuts, lightly toasted then roughly chopped
2 courgettes, spiralized or julienned

To serve
a few coriander leaves
1 lime, halved
2 tbsp Sweet Chilli Dipping Sauce (see page 116)

In a small bowl, combine the soy sauce, spring onions, cornflour and garlic. Chop the thighs into bite-sized chunks and add them to the marinade. Marinate for about 10 minutes, or cover the bowl with clingfilm and marinate in the fridge overnight.

In a wok or large frying pan, heat the oil over a high heat, then sauté the chicken mixture for about 10 minutes, or until cooked. Keep the heat medium-high and keep the chicken moving around the wok for a few minutes until the chicken is coloured.

Toss the cashews through the dish for a minute, then transfer to a large bowl and toss through the courgette noodles. If you like your noodles cooked, then add to the wok and sauté in the juices that are left in the pan.

Serve with lime, coriander and the Sweet Chilli Dipping Sauce.

FAT (g): 28.6
PROTEIN (g): 49.6
CARBS (g): 57.1
FIBRE (g): 11.5
CALORIES: 708
SERVES: 2 (MAKES 4 KOFTE)

This dish is my all-time favourite. The lamb kebab gets a healthier twist here with lots of high-volume, low-calorie veggies and lean minced lamb.

LAMB KOFTE WITH GREEK SALAD

300g lamb mince
1 small bunch of mint, finely chopped (use 1 tbsp here and save the rest for sprinkling)
1 tsp ground cumin
1 garlic clove, finely chopped
½ red onion, very finely chopped
salt and pepper
1 tsp smoked paprika
½ tsp olive oil

For the Greek salad
6 vine tomatoes, cut into chunks
½ red onion, thinly sliced
juice of 1 lime
salt and pepper
50g mixed olives
1 cucumber, halved, deseeded and sliced
80g feta cheese, crumbled
a few basil leaves, torn

To serve
dried red chilli flakes, for sprinkling
2 lemon wedges
2 tbsp Greek yogurt
2 wholemeal pitta breads

Put the lamb mince, mint, cumin, garlic, onion, salt and pepper and paprika in a bowl and scrunch together with your hands until evenly combined. Roll into 4 long, thin sausages. You can cook these straightaway or chill them for up to 24 hours.

When you're ready to cook the kofte, preheat a frying pan until very hot, then reduce the heat to medium-high, add the olive oil, then the kofte and cook for 3–4 minutes on each side. Don't turn until they are well sealed or the meat will stick to the pan. Cook them for about 10 minutes in total.

Meanwhile, for the Greek salad, simply add all the ingredients to a bowl and gently toss to combine.

Serve the koftas with the salad, chilli flakes, lemon wedges, yogurt, pitta bread and a sprinkling of mint.

FAT (g): 6.8
PROTEIN (g): 29.9
CARBS (g): 69.3
FIBRE (g): 17.4
CALORIES: 493
SERVES: 2

This wholesome classic is given a veggie twist with fibre-, iron- and protein-rich black lentils. I've given two variations for the rice base, so you can choose which one you prefer based on your macros for the day. If I've trained, I will choose the basmati; if not, I'll choose the cauliflower, as the chilli is already carb-rich. Serve this to your guests with the Spicy Avocado Dip on page 80 and some corn chips. The cauliflower rice saves you about 20g carbs over the basmati while adding fibre and volume to the dish. If you have time, the sweet onions from the recipe on page 85 work particularly well stirred through the cauliflower rice.

ONE-POT BLACK LENTIL CHILLI WITH SPICY CAULIFLOWER RICE

1 tsp coconut oil
1 red onion, finely diced
2 garlic cloves, chopped or grated
1 chilli, deseeded (optional) or ½ tsp dried red chilli flakes
1 tsp ground cumin
1 tsp thyme (fresh or dried)
1 tbsp chipotle paste
200g black lentils, rinsed
400g can chopped tomatoes
100ml vegetable stock or water
salt and pepper

For the spicy cauliflower rice
200g cauliflower
1 tsp coconut oil
salt and pepper
1 tsp ground cumin
1 tsp smoked paprika
pinch of dried red chilli flakes
1 tbsp finely chopped jalapeños

To serve
basmati rice (200g cooked weight), optional
1 tbsp chopped coriander, for sprinkling

Heat a large saucepan over a medium heat until hot, add the oil, then the onion and garlic. Reduce the heat and sauté for 8 minutes. Add the chilli, cumin, thyme and chipotle and stir to combine. Add the rinsed lentils, tomatoes, stock or water and a good pinch of salt and pepper. Bring to the boil briefly, cover with a lid, reduce the heat and simmer for 40 minutes, or until the lentils are tender. If you prefer a thicker chilli, uncover for the last 10 minutes to let some of the liquid evaporate.

For the spicy cauliflower rice, grate or pulse the cauliflower until it resembles rice. Heat the oil in a large frying pan or saucepan over a medium-high heat, then add the cauliflower with a splash of water and the remaining ingredients. Cover with a lid and steam for 4 minutes, stirring occasionally to make sure the rice doesn't stick.

Spoon the chilli over the cauliflower rice (or cooked basmati rice) and top with coriander to serve.

FAT (g): 36
PROTEIN (g): 34.8
CARBS (g): 26.4
FIBRE (g): 8.7
CALORIES: 587
SERVES: 4

This is a family recipe handed down to my from my nana Perveen, who has been making me this dish my whole life. Everyone I make it for says it's the best curry they've ever had. It's definitely a banquet dish, so I would put it in a large serving dish for everyone to dig in alongside the potatoes, the salsa and the raita from page 87. The good news is, after the initial prep you can leave it cooking for a few hours, allowing you time with your guests. Most of the spices in this recipe we have used through the book, so you should have them in your cupboards.

SAG GOSHT, CORIANDER SALSA & BOMBAY SWEET POTATOES

Heat the oil in a large saucepan over a high heat. Season the meat liberally with salt and pepper, add to the pan and seal on all sides until golden brown. Scoop out the meat, reduce the heat to medium-low and add the onions, garlic, ginger and chilli and sauté for about 8 minutes. Increase the heat again, then add the mustard seeds, fenugreek, garam masala, cardamom seeds, cumin, coriander and turmeric and stir until everything is coated and the mustard seeds start popping. Immediately add the meat back to the pan followed by the tomatoes and stock. Bring to the boil, cover, reduce the heat to low and simmer for 3 hours. Alternatively, put into an oven preheated to 150°C/gas mark 2 and cook for 3 hours. Make sure the pan is ovenproof. You can also use a slow cooker.

Steam the spinach for a minute or so, then wring out in a clean tea towel or leave to drain on kitchen paper. Place the spinach in a food processor and blitz or finely chop by hand, then stir into the curry about 30 minutes before the end of the cooking time.

When ready to serve, if the meat is on the bone carefully shred the meat off the bone and pull apart in the sauce with 2 forks. If your curry is a little drier, then uncover 30 minutes before the end to thicken and entice your guests with the wonderful aromas.

1 tsp coconut oil
600g boned shoulder of lamb
salt and pepper
2 onions, sliced or finely chopped
2 garlic cloves, chopped
5cm piece of fresh root ginger, peeled and grated
1 red chilli, deseeded (optional) and finely chopped
1 tsp mustard seeds (optional)
½ tsp ground fenugreek (optional)
1 tsp garam masala
2 cardamom pods, lightly crushed to release seeds
1 tsp cumin (seeds or ground it doesn't matter)
1 tsp ground coriander
1 tsp ground turmeric
400g can of chopped tomatoes
200ml lamb or vegetable stock
100g spinach

For the Bombay sweet potatoes
2 tbsp coconut oil
1 tsp mustard seeds
½ tsp chilli powder
½ tsp ground turmeric
300g potatoes, parboiled for a few minutes and
    cut into 2.5cm cubes
salt

For the coriander salsa
1 large bunch of coriander
2.5cm piece of fresh root ginger, peeled
1 green chilli, deseeded (optional)
salt and pepper
juice of 2 lemons or limes
about 50ml water
pinch of ground cumin (optional)

"If you can't get boned lamb, buy it on the bone but with a total weight of 1kg. You will have to take the meat off the bone when the curry is ready to serve."

For the Bombay sweet potatoes, heat the oil in a pan over a medium-high heat. Sprinkle in the mustard seeds and when they begin to pop, add the chilli and turmeric. Fry for 1 minute, then add the potatoes and fry until the edges begin to get crisp and golden, about 4–5 minutes Add a good pinch of salt, cover with a lid and cook over a medium heat for a further 5 minutes, or until the potatoes are tender.

For the coriander salsa, simply blitz all the ingredients together in a mini food processor or blender until smooth.

Serve the curry topped with a sprinkle of garam masala, if you like and with the potatoes and salsa on the side. As a banquet meal this is wonderful served with a chopped tomato, cucumber and red onion salad with lots of fresh lime. Flavour without the calories.

FAT (g): 8.5
PROTEIN (g): 21.1
CARBS (g): 12.3
FIBRE (g): 4.7
CALORIES: 220
SERVES: 2

When recipe testing this, I must have eaten four bowlfuls while tweaking the sauce. When I logged what I'd eaten into MyFitnessPal afterwards I was shocked to see it was fewer calories and carbs than ONE bowl made with pasta. Courgetti gets a lot of stick for being trendy, but… if I can save 125 calories and 29g carbs while keeping some fibre and adding vitamins simply by replacing 100g cooked pasta with 100g courgette AND still getting that al dente texture then HELL YES I'm trendy! If you have a little more time, it's nice to make your own tomato sauce with fresh tomato but a good-quality can is absolutely fine here and makes this a speedy supper, ready in under 20 minutes.

LOW-CARB ITALIAN CHILLI CRAB 'PASTA'

1 tbsp olive oil
2 shallots, finely diced
2 garlic cloves, finely chopped
1 red chilli, deseeded (optional) and finely chopped
4 tbsp white wine
50g brown crabmeat
400g can good-quality Italian chopped tomatoes
salt and pepper
100g white crabmeat
juice of 1 lemon
1 large handful of flat leaf parsley, finely chopped
2 medium courgettes, spiralized or julienned

Heat the olive oil in a medium saucepan over a medium heat and sauté the shallots, garlic and chilli for about 8 minutes. Increase the heat to high, add the wine and when it begins bubbling and reducing add the brown crabmeat. Stir quickly, then add the tomatoes and a good pinch of salt and pepper and simmer, uncovered, for about 10 minutes, or longer if you have time.

When you're ready to serve, add the white crabmeat, lemon juice and parsley and toss through to make sure it's all evenly combined. Toss through the courgettes right before serving.

FAT (g): 6.8
PROTEIN (g): 27.5
CARBS (g): 33.9
FIBRE (g): 7.4
CALORIES: 322
SERVES: 2

This is a quick, light supper that I enjoy alfresco with friends and a small glass of chilled wine. Buckwheat is a SIRT food; it's claimed that these special foods work by activating specific proteins in the body called sirutins, which are believed to protect cells in the body from dying when they are under stress. They are thought to regulate inflammation and metabolism. Get the best prawns you can afford with this – some fishmongers have bags of frozen tiger prawns which, when shelled and cleaned, are fat and juicy, and my preference for this dish. Chop and change the veg to whatever you prefer – broccoli, baby corn and sugar snaps are great alternatives.

ASIAN KING PRAWN STIR-FRY WITH BUCKWHEAT NOODLES

50g buckwheat noodles
1 tsp toasted sesame oil or olive oil
2 tsp olive oil
2.5cm piece of fresh root ginger, peeled and grated
2 garlic cloves, finely chopped
1 small chilli, chopped and deseeded if preferred
4 spring onions, finely sliced
1 red pepper, thinly sliced
85g water chestnuts
85g bamboo shoots
100g beansprouts
1 head of pak choi, cut in half lengthways
1 tbsp tamari or soy sauce
1 tbsp fish sauce
juice of 1 lime
1 tsp coconut sugar or soft brown sugar
1 bunch of coriander
200g raw tiger prawns, shelled and deveined

To serve
lime wedges
chopped coriander, for sprinkling

This is a super-quick dish, so cook the noodles first according to the packet instructions and toss them in the sesame or olive oil to stop them sticking while you prepare the stir-fry.

Heat 1 tsp of the olive oil in a wok over a medium heat, add the ginger, garlic, chilli and spring onions and stir-fry for 1 minute. Increase the heat to high, add the red pepper, water chestnuts, bamboo shoots, beansprouts and pak choi and toss together until the pak choi starts to wilt. Remove from the heat and add the tamari, fish sauce, lime juice and sugar and toss until coated. Tip into a serving dish.

Heat the remaining 1 tsp oil in the wok a high heat, add the prawns and toss for 1–2 minutes until they turn pink, then tip onto the vegetables.

Serve over the noodles with extra lime for squeezing over and a sprinkle of coriander.

GRAB
& GO

Designed with a busy working life in mind, these 'grab & go' dishes are portable and last for a while in airtight containers. They are quick to prepare, convenient to pack and deliciously moreish – packable snacks for a healthier you.
I can't tell you the number of times I've had to eat something that I wasn't happy with because I was travelling and didn't have access to healthier options. Being prepared is key to helping you stay on track.

FAT (g): 8.4
PROTEIN (g): 21
CARBS (g): 26.8
FIBRE (g): 4.1
CALORIES: 275
SERVES: 1

It is especially important to consume protein after a workout, as during exercise you are effectively breaking down your muscles and protein helps to rebuild them. Do have a quickly digestible protein shake at the gym if you like, however choose a good-quality whey protein or vegetarian equivalent with no added sugars and consume your shake (or your next meal) as soon as you can after working out. Remember to factor the protein shake into your daily macros and only have it if you need it as a snack or portable meal – not as an extra. My ultimate post-workout shake is excellent for breakfast, too, and takes just 2 minutes to whizz up.

MY ULTIMATE POST-WORKOUT SHAKE

"Banana replenishes the body's glycogen stores but leave it out if you're on the Kickstart plan, as it may take you over your carb allowance."

150ml unsweetened almond milk (or milk of choice but don't forget to add to your macros)
1 small banana (about 100–120g), chopped and frozen
1 scoop of protein powder (it should be around 100cals and 25g protein with less than 5g carbs)
10g peanut butter (about 1 heaped tsp)
1 tsp chia seeds
few ice cubes

Whizz all the ingredients in the best blender you have. The banana doesn't have to be frozen but makes the shake super-thick and tasty and serve.

FAT (g): 16.2
PROTEIN (g): 9.1
CARBS (g): 5.7
FIBRE (g): 2.8
CALORIES: 210
MAKES: 6 SERVINGS

This is my ultimate snack. I make a huge batch of these and keep them in an airtight container for snacking. They also add a great texture to a simple salad. I usually throw these in the bottom of the oven on a Sunday when I'm cooking something else at the same temperature. The recipe works with chickpeas, too.

SPICY CRUNCHY BAKED SEEDS

1 tsp coconut oil
1 tbsp tamari
100g pumpkin seeds
100g sunflower seeds
1 tsp cayenne pepper
1 tsp smoked paprika

Alternative flavour combos
1 tbsp miso paste
1 tbsp low-salt Cajun seasoning

Preheat the oven to 150°C/gas mark 2 and line a baking tray with baking paper.

Melt the coconut oil, then pour into a small bowl, add the tamari and whisk together. Toss this mixture through the seeds in another bowl. It'll only just coat them but that's what we want. Sprinkle over the spices and toss to coat again before tipping into the prepared baking tray. Bake in the oven for 40 minutes until brown and crunchy, shaking the tray a few times through the cooking time.

NOTE

If you're using the miso paste, melt it in 1 tbsp boiling water before coating the seeds.

FAT (g): 8
PROTEIN (g): 19.6
CARBS (g): 58.2
FIBRE (g): 11.9
CALORIES: 407
SERVES: 1

This is a hug in a bowl. The broth is reheated in minutes as long as you have access to a kettle on your travels. Chop and change the veg to your taste but I love the meaty textures of this combo. If you're on the Kickstart plan, leave out the rice to make this a high-volume, low-calorie meal. The leftover veggies from the ingredients list can be transformed into the Thai Poached Salmon Bowl (see page 112) for dinner. If you can't get black rice, don't worry – basmati works here too, but black rice is deliciously nutty and full of phytonutrients, which are a good source of fibre.

CHUNKY NOURISHING MISO BROTH WITH BLACK RICE

"You can get ahead by preparing a few of these containers and storing them in the fridge for the week."

½ tsp coconut oil
½ onion, finely diced
50g shiitake or chestnut mushrooms
2.5cm piece of fresh root ginger, peeled and finely diced or grated
½ garlic clove, finely chopped
1 head of pak choi, chopped
75g beansprouts (about ¼ pack)
1 medium carrot, cut into matchsticks
50g edamame (pop the rest of the bag in the freezer for another day)
2 tbsp brown rice miso paste
1 small handful of coriander, leaves only
1 chilli, chopped, or ½ tsp dried red chilli flakes
100g cooked black rice, to serve
200ml boiling water

In a frying pan, heat the oil over a medium-high heat, then add the onion and mushrooms and sauté until the mushrooms are golden, about 10 minutes. Add the ginger and garlic and fry for 1 minute, then tip into an airtight container.

Quickly sauté the pak choi in the same pan for a minute or so, then tip into your container. Add the carrots to the pan with a splash of water, cover and steam for a few minutes until they are cooked to your liking. Drain and tip into the container with the edamame, miso paste, coriander and chilli.

When you're ready to eat, simply add the boiling water to the container, whisk, shake or stir to mix up all the ingredients and eat. The warm broth will reheat the veggies perfectly.

FAT (g): 8.6
PROTEIN (g): 2.5
CARBS (g): 5.4
FIBRE (g): 2.6
CALORIES: 114
MAKES: 24

These 'grab & go' sweet treats hit the spot while packing in the nutrients. They are particularly good frozen, so keep a stash for those cravings. They're perfect on the Kickstart plan as a meal replacement with My Ultimate Post-Workout Shake (page 148).

RAW VEGAN TAHINI GOJI BITES

300g medjool dates
60g sesame seeds, lightly toasted until golden
160g desiccated coconut, lightly toasted until golden
120g tahini
1 tsp vanilla extract
1 tsp salt
50g goji berries

If the dates are not soft and juicy then soak them in warm water for about 10 minutes. Drain.

Place the dates in a food processor and whizz until smooth, then add the sesame seeds, coconut, tahini, vanilla and salt and whizz again until quite smooth. Tip out into a bowl and stir or scrunch the goji berries into the mix. Take small pieces of the mix and roll into balls. Arrange on a tray and refrigerate for a few hours or freeze for 30 minutes to set.

FAT (g): 33.5
PROTEIN (g): 50
CARBS (g): 11.9
FIBRE (g): 9.6
CALORIES: 568
SERVES: 1

Pronounced 'poh-keh', these are all the rage in health-conscious LA. They are super bowls packed with veggies and lean protein. The sauce in my version is lighter than the classic, which usually features mayonnaise. Poke are great on the Kickstart plan, as they're high volume and low calorie. Chop and change the veggies to your taste. Seaweed is traditional (I recommend dried wakame or hijiki) but it isn't everyone's cuppa, so leave it out if you prefer. For the pickled ginger, get hold of the little sachets whenever you come across them and keep them in the fridge for times like these when you only need a little.

TUNA POKE

½ medium avocado, cut into 1cm cubes
¼ head of iceberg lettuce, finely shredded
4 radishes, very thinly sliced
½ cucumber, very thinly sliced
150g sashimi-grade tuna steak, cut into 1cm cubes
1 spring onion, finely sliced
2 tbsp sesame seeds, lightly toasted (black and white are nice)
pickled ginger sachet
few coriander stalks, finely chopped
1 tsp honey
1 tsp toasted sesame oil
2 tbsp tamari or soy sauce
1 tsp Sriracha, wasabi or any low sugar hot sauce (optional)
juice and finely grated zest of 1 lime

Throw the veggies in an airtight container or arrange nicely in a bowl. Add the diced tuna to one side and sprinkle over the spring onion, sesame seeds, pickled ginger and coriander.

Make the dressing in another small container by whisking the honey, sesame oil, tamari or soy sauce, Sriracha and lime zest and juice together.

Just before you're ready to eat, tip the dressing over the tuna, stir and leave for 5 minutes for the flavours to mingle and the lime to cook the tuna a little.

FAT (g): 20
PROTEIN (g): 17.8
CARBS (g): 15.1
FIBRE (g): 0.7
CALORIES: 312
SERVES: 2

Halloumi fries are my ultimate quick comfort food. I love them on days where my carbs are low and I'm allowed a little more fat. It's a great barbecue side, too. There's no need to deep-fry them – my recipe uses a little oil and still yields a crispy chip.

HALLOUMI FRIES WITH CHIPOTLE YOGURT

2 tbsp coconut oil for shallow-frying
2 tbsp plain flour, gluten-free flour or chickpea flour
110g halloumi (about ½ pack), cut into long rectangles

For the salt sprinkles
1 tsp sea salt flakes
1 tsp chopped rosemary

For the chipotle yogurt
1 tsp chipotle paste
pinch of smoked paprika (optional)
4 tbsp natural yogurt
juice of 1 lemon or lime

Heat the oil in a frying pan until very hot but not smoking. Spread the flour out on a plate and dust the halloumi fries in the flour, patting off any excess. Carefully place the fries in the oil and cook for 1 minute on each side side until crisp and golden, then remove and drain on kitchen paper.

For the salt sprinkles, mix the salt and rosemary together and sprinkle over the fries while they are still warm.

For the chipotle yogurt, stir the chipotle and paprika into the yogurt and add enough lemon or lime juice to taste.

Serve the fries with the yogurt. Add a large, green leafy salad for lunch, or some lean protein for dinner.

FAT (g): 24.4
PROTEIN (g): 17.4
CARBS (g): 20.5
FIBRE (g): 6.2
CALORIES: 383
SERVES: 1

Be the envy of the work mates with your colourful Instagram-worthy creation. Mix and match these super salad jars for a different flavour and colour combo every day. Pick one of each and never eat the same lunch twice while enjoying a host of health benefits. Stick to my weight recommendations thoughout the recipe and remember to log the macros. No assembly instructions needed – just layer up your ingredients!

"The nutritional breakdown given here is for a jar layered with quinoa, tofu, pine nuts, herbs, tomatoes, cucumber, red pepper, spring onions and harissa dressing."

DIY SALAD JAR SHAKERS

Base: 50g
canned chickpeas, drained
canned black beans, drained
cooked lentils
cooked quinoa
cooked brown rice
shredded romaine or iceberg lettuce
thinly sliced red cabbage
roast squash (get adventurous with spices)
crispy kale (or just marinated or steamed)

Veggies: no weight – just fit in as many as you can
diced red onion, macerated in lime juice
carrot noodles or batons
courgette noodles
sugar snap peas or mangetout
radish
diced cucumber
diced roast pepper
sweetcorn
sautéed drained spinach (or raw)
tomatoes

Fat: 25g
feta cheese
torn mozzarella
nuts (try chopped smoked almonds – they are amazing)
olives
boiled egg
avocado
toasted pine nuts

Protein: 100g
Use your imagination, but leftovers are great here as well as marinated tofu and diced chorizo or bacon.

Topping:
herbs
soft salad leaves (these are better on top so they don't squish)
portion of the Spicy Crunchy Baked Seeds (see page 149)

Dressing: 2 tbsp
I like to keep the dressings light and vinegar-, herb-, citrus-based instead of oil-based.
Sweet Chilli Dipping Sauce (see page 116)
harissa paste, thinned with lemon juice
Greek yogurt, thinned with lemon juice and 1 tsp ground turmeric, salt and pepper
pesto thinned with water and lemon juice to make a runny dressing

FAT (g): 14.7
PROTEIN (g): 23.2
CARBS (g): 4.7
FIBRE (g): 1.7
CALORIES: 247
MAKES: 12 (6 PORTIONS)

Many a time I've been in a train station at 8A.M. with the choice of a stale croissant or a bar of chocolate, wishing I'd made these frittatas the night before. They take under 30 minutes to make and yield a few days' worth of breakfast, lunch or 'grab & go' snacks. Lean protein, super-low carbs, lots of veggies with some healthy fats, too. Finish with a squeeze of lemon, however you enjoy them, to help your body absorb the plant-based iron in the spinach.

PROTEIN MUFFIN FRITTATAS

low-cal fry spray, for greasing
50g spinach (about ½ a bag)
1 small onion, very finely diced
12 eggs
1 tsp pesto of choice
100ml semi-skimmed milk
1 tsp dried oregano
salt and pepper
1 red pepper, very finely diced
1 courgette, very finely diced
200g lean ham, roughly chopped
100g feta cheese, crumbled
12 cherry tomatoes, halved

Preheat the oven to 200°C/gas mark 6 and use low-cal fry spray to grease a deep 12-hole cupcake or muffin tin. Alternatively, line with muffin cases.

Spray a frying pan large enough to fit all the spinach with the low-cal fry spray, then add the spinach and sauté over a medium heat for 1 minute until wilted. Drain and squeeze in a clean tea towel to remove any excess moisture. Add the onion to the pan and sauté for a few minutes until starting to soften.

Crack the eggs into a bowl, add the pesto, milk, oregano salt and pepper and whisk well to combine. Pour the mixture into the muffin tin until each hole is half full. Chop or tear the spinach into 12 portions and add a little to each hole. Repeat this process with the onion, pepper, courgette and ham, then top with a little feta and 2 tomato halves.

Reduce the oven temperature to 190°C/gas mark 5 and bake for 20 minutes until set and golden.

Allow to cool, then divide them into portions and cover with clingfilm. Chill until you need them. Either have them as they are, on the go, or enjoy with a large, green leafy salad.

FAT (g): 11.7
PROTEIN (g): 26.7
CARBS (g): 12.9
FIBRE (g): 6.6
CALORIES: 277
MAKES: 2 PORTIONS

This is an amazing, quick-to-prepare portable dipper that's loaded with protein from a variety of sources. Try it with a portion of corn tortillas or two small toasted wholemeal pitta breads for lunch. Using smoked salmon trimmings keeps this super cheap, too, while packing in the flavour. Leave out the yogurt, if you like, but it does add volume, protein and a creamy texture.

SMOKED SALMON & CANNELLINI BEAN DIP

150g smoked salmon trimmings
175g canned cannellini beans
50g Greek yogurt
few tbsp coriander, dill, tarragon, whatever you like, finely chopped
finely grated zest and juice of 1 lemon
¼ garlic clove (optional)
1 tbsp sesame seeds, lightly toasted (black and white are nice)
salt and pepper

This is super easy: whizz all the ingredients in a food processor, a high-speed blender or mini-chopper and season to taste. If you don't have a machine, just mash the beans and finely chop the salmon and mix it all together in a bowl.

Keep in an airtight container for 2 days and freshen up with a squeeze of lemon juice before serving.

FAT (g): 18.3
PROTEIN (g): 13.2
CARBS (g): 20.1
FIBRE (g): 3.7
CALORIES: 305
SERVES: 6

Sometimes a bit of luxury on a diet is needed. No matter how hard we try, once in a while the cravings won't subside. This is my version of a quiche which I have lightened to suit any of the meal plans. My version saves you a whopping 200 calories per serving over a traditional quiche: that's half the calories for what I hope is a very similar flavour. I use chestnut flour as it's gluten free, high in protein and has a lovely nutty flavour. A top speed-up tip is to use individual, deep disposable foil tins, which are amazing at cooking the pastry without the need for blind baking, saving you a lot of time and hassle. If you can't handle dairy, substitute the butter, milk and cheese for dairy-free options which are readily available. The macros will be pretty similar so don't stress trying to recalculate them.

QUICHE WITH CHESTNUT CRUST

60g cold butter, cubed
150g chestnut flour
1½ tsp dried oregano or herbes de Provence
pinch of salt
1 large egg, lightly beaten

For the filling
6 eggs, lightly beaten
100ml semi-skimmed milk
salt and pepper
1 tsp coconut oil
1 onion, sliced
1 garlic clove, finely chopped
mix of chopped veggies such as tomatoes, courgette, peppers, spinach, kale, roast aubergine, mushrooms, asparagus, olives
50g reduced-fat mature Cheddar cheese, grated

Preheat the oven to 190°C/gas mark 5.

Using a food processor, pulse the butter into the flour, herbs and salt – around 10 pulses should do it. Then use the egg to bind the mixture; you might not need it all. Once it has come together into a dough, remove from the machine and divide into 6 balls (for individual tartlets) or 2 (for medium quiches). Roll out each ball and use to line whichever sized tins you are using.

For the filling, whisk the eggs, milk, salt and pepper together with a fork.

Heat the coconut oil in a frying pan and sauté the onion and garlic for about 8 minutes until soft and sweet. Sprinkle the onion and garlic into the quiche tins first, then fill with your favourite veggies. Don't overfill. Pour over the egg mixture and sprinkle with the cheese. Bake in the oven for 15–20 minutes until puffed up, golden and cooked through.

NOTE

Freeze whatever you don't eat over the next few days.

DESSERTS

We all need a treat every now and again, but how can we achieve that on a diet while not going mad on the calories? This chapter has a few great dessert recipes with lots of scope to tweak and transform to your own taste. They won't set back your hard work, but will satisfy those cravings while providing nutritional value. (I promise, if you reach for the chocolate bar it won't satisfy you and you'll want something else in five minutes.)

FAT (g): 16.7
PROTEIN (g): 6.7
CARBS (g): 19.2
FIBRE (g): 2.1
CALORIES: 258
MAKES: 12 SERVINGS

Another hit from my Eat Naked café, this is high in fibre and slow-release carbohydrates – wonderful for breakfast or after you have trained to help replace glycogen stores. Keep your portion control strict and maybe bulk out with some Greek yogurt and fresh fruit. This is suitable for freezing, as I don't expect you to eat all 12 slices in one go. It's also wonderful toasted.

BANANA BREAD

6 tbsp coconut oil, melted
4 eggs
100g Sukrin (a sugar substitute that contains no carbs and is available from most supermarkets and healthfood shops)
4 tbsp coconut cream
1 tsp vanilla extract
pinch of salt
½ tsp bicarbonate of soda
125g wholegrain gluten-free flour
125g ground almonds
5 medium over-ripe bananas (about 600g) total mashed
4 tbsp flaked almonds

Preheat the oven to 180°C/gas mark 4 and grease a 700g loaf tin with a tiny amount of the melted coconut oil.

Beat the eggs and Sukrin for a few minutes until pale and thick using electric beaters or a freestanding electric mixer. Add the coconut oil, coconut cream, vanilla and salt and beat briefly to combine. Fold in the bicarbonate of soda, flour, ground almonds and the mashed bananas.

Spoon the mixture into the prepared loaf tin until it is about 1cm from the top of the tin. Sprinkle the flaked almonds on top and bake in the oven for 50 minutes but check it after 40 minutes. The loaf should be well risen, golden and a skewer inserted into the middle should come out clean.

Remove the tin from the oven and run a knife around the loaf while it's still warm to make it easier to take out of the tin. Leave to cool for a few minutes, then remove from the tin and transfer to a wire rack to cool completely. Keep in an airtight container in the fridge for 3 days.

If freezing, wrap well in clingfilm and defrost on a plate in the fridge overnight.

FAT (g): 13.5
PROTEIN (g): 8.1
CARBS (g): 21.9
FIBRE (g): 3.9
CALORIES: 249
MAKES: 8

Think of these as a modern granola bar but loaded with nutrients and slow-release carbs, helping you to feel fuller for longer, and natural energy-boosting ingredients – all with the natural sweetness from fruit and no nasty added refined sugars. If you're someone who reaches for the biscuit tin at 11A.M. you'll love these hearty, soft baked and chewy bars. They are really adaptable so feel free to play around with the extras.

MIGHTY BARS

2 medium bananas, mashed
4 tbsp peanut butter
1 tsp vanilla extract
pinch of salt
100g jumbo oats (optional)
60g dried cranberries
25g walnuts
40g sunflower seeds
40g pumpkin seeds
30g flaked almonds
1 tsp mixed spice

Preheat the oven to 180°C/gas mark 4 and line a 8 x 8cm baking tin with baking paper.

Using your hands, scrunch all the ingredients together in a large bowl until combined. Spoon the mixture into the prepared tin and, using lightly damp hands, firmly press and smooth out evenly. Bake in the oven for 20–25 minutes until firm and lightly brown. They'll firm up once set, so don't overbake them. Remove from the oven and allow to cool.

Once cool, remove the baked slab from the tin and slice into 8 bars. Wrap in clingfilm and freeze for up to 1 month, or store in the fridge for up to 1 week.

FAT (g): 12.3
PROTEIN (g): 12.9
CARBS (g): 12.1
FIBRE (g): 3.2
CALORIES: 217
SERVES: 1

These are whipped up and eaten within literally seconds – a chocolatey hit that will satisfy that late-night craving when you usually nip to the off-licence for a family-sized chocolate bar… or is that just me?! It's super-low carb, too.

2-MINUTE NAUGHTY POTS

1 egg white
1 tsp raw cacao or cocoa powder
pinch of salt
1 tsp vanilla extract
2 tbsp ground almonds (or ½ scoop of chocolate or vanilla protein powder)
3 tbsp almond milk or milk of choice
tiny pinch of bicarbonate of soda
1 tsp honey

To serve
1 tbsp Greek yogurt
1 tbsp raspberries, to serve

Whisk all the ingredients together in a large mug with a fork until smooth, then microwave on full power for 90 seconds. Serve straight from the mug with Greek yogurt and raspberries.

FAT (g): 15.4
PROTEIN (g): 2.8
CARBS (g): 4.9
FIBRE (g): 4.3
CALORIES: 178
SERVES: 2

"I promise you won't be able to taste the avocado in this!"

This is the base of so many desserts at my café. It can be transformed into chocolate orange with orange zest and orange blossom water, or add some raspberries or a few Kirsch-soaked cherries, or 1 tsp cacao nibs for crunch, or a shot of espresso for a kick (coffee and chocolate are best mates). All of these tweaks elevate this simple dessert while adding very few calories. This dish fits into lots of popular diets, as it's so low carb while loading in the healthy fats, vitamins and minerals.

AVOCADO CACAO MOUSSE

1 ripe avocado
2 tbsp raw cacao or cocoa powder
1 tsp honey or maple
1 tsp vanilla extract
tiny pinch of salt

Blend all the ingredients together in a mini food processor until smooth, then spoon into 2 little bowls. Chill if you can as they are better cold and firm, but if you can't wait they are just as good straight out the blender. Cover the one you don't eat with clingfilm and keep it in the fridge for up to 3 days.

FAT (g): 6.3
PROTEIN (g): 2.5
CARBS (g): 12.7
FIBRE (g): 1.3
CALORIES: 120
MAKES: 8

These are moreish little bites I stash in the freezer and bake when I need them. They are great as a snack, too, when travelling. These cookies are lower in sugar than you would expect. Don't use coconut flour here, as it doesn't work. A mix of all three seeds is nice but if you can only get one, use sesame.

SUPER-SEED COOKIES

1 tbsp tahini
1 tbsp maple syrup or coconut sugar
1 tbsp coconut oil melted
good pinch of salt
1 tsp vanilla extract
100g gluten-free flour
1 tbsp sesame seeds
1 tbsp flaxseeds (linseeds)
1 tbsp sunflower seeds

Preheat the oven to 180°C/gas mark 4.

The cookies are best made a mini food processor, as the dough comes together nicely this way. In the food processor, blend the tahini, maple syrup, coconut oil, salt and vanilla, and flour.

The mix will be firm but that's what you are looking for. Portion the mixture into 8 pieces and roll into balls, then place on a baking tray and pat down with your hands to flatten slightly. Top with the seeds or dip the cookie discs into the seeds for a good coating. Now's the time to freeze any cookies that you don't plan to bake – just wrap them in clingfilm and freeze for up to 1 month.

Bake the cookies in the oven for 8–10 minutes. They will firm up once cooled do don't overbake them. Remove from the oven and allow to cool.

Keep them in an airtight container, preferably in the freezer otherwise you maybe tempted to munch them all in one go.

FAT (g): 26.5
PROTEIN (g): 7
CARBS (g): 12.2
FIBRE (g): 3
CALORIES: 321
SERVES: 8

Sometimes you just need a bit of cake. This is a fresh, tropical flavour that's great for taking to an event where you'll be tempted to indulge – at least then you can indulge and stick to your goals.

COCONUT LIME LOAF CAKE

100g coconut oil, melted
100g ground almonds
100g Sukrin (a sugar substitute that contains no carbs and is available from most supermarkets and healthfood shops)
100g gluten-free flour
50g desiccated coconut
½ tsp baking powder
pinch of salt
1 tsp vanilla extract
finely grated zest of 3 limes
3 eggs
120ml coconut milk
2 tbsp flaked coconut, for sprinkling

To serve
1 tbsp coconut yogurt
finely grated lime zest

Preheat the oven to 180°C/gas mark 4 and grease a 450g loaf tin measuring 16 x 10cm, and 7cm deep with a tiny amount of the melted coconut oil. Line the base with a strip of baking paper to make it easier to lift out.

Mix the ground almonds, Sukrin, flour, desiccated coconut, baking powder, salt, vanilla and lime zest together in a bowl.

In a separate bowl, whisk the eggs with the milk and coconut oil.

Fold the wet ingredients into the dry ingredients. Spoon the mixture into the prepared tin and sprinkle with the flaked coconut. Bake in the oven for about 40 minutes until risen, golden and firm to the touch.

Allow to cool in the tin for 5 minutes, then serve with coconut yogurt flecked with extra lime zest.

NOTE

If you don't have a small loaf tin with the right dimensions, make this in a standard loaf tin. The cake will be shallower so it will cook more quickly – check it after 20 minutes in the oven.

FAT (g): 15.8
PROTEIN (g): 4.3
CARBS (g): 14.1
FIBRE (g): 4.8
CALORIES: 225
SERVES: 6

This cake is a sneaky raw treat. There's no cooking involved at all, it's loaded with fresh veggies, and the frosting is made with cashew nuts. So this is dairy free, gluten free and also free of refined sugars.

RAW CARROT CAKE WITH CREAMY CASHEW FROSTING

160g carrots, grated
1 medium apple, grated
100g medjool dates, pitted
1 tsp vanilla extract
1 tsp mixed spice
pinch of salt
4 tbsp desiccated coconut, toasted
50g walnuts, lightly toasted, then roughly chopped

For the frosting
50g cashew nuts
50g coconut cream (the hard part from the top of a can)
1 tsp honey
1 tsp vanilla extract
finely grated zest of 1 orange
1 tbsp coconut oil, melted
1 tsp ground cinnamon, for sprinkling

Soak the cashew nuts for the frosting in a bowl of cold water for 4 hours. Alternatively, soak them in warm water for 1 hour, then drain and set aside.

If the dates are not soft and juicy then soak them in warm water for about 10 minutes. Drain.

Line a 15–18cm square tin with baking paper.

For the cake, place the grated carrots and apple in a tea towel and squeeze out any excess moisture. There will be quite a bit of liquid so do it over the sink.

Blend the dates in a mini food processor to a purée and transfer to a bowl. Add the carrot, apple, vanilla, salt, spice, coconut and walnuts and scrunch the mixture together with your hands. Press the mixture down firmly into the prepared tin and set aside. The mixture will feel wet – this is normal.

The frosting is really easy! Simply whizz all the ingredients, including the soaked cashews, together in a food processor until smooth. Spread the frosting over the cake and refrigerate for at least 4 hours until the cake is set and the frosting has firmed up.

To serve, lift the cake out of the tin and sprinkle with more cinnamon.

FAT (g): 9.2
PROTEIN (g): 1.7
CARBS (g): 0.8
FIBRE (g): 2.3
CALORIES: 98
MAKES: 8

Wicked on the Kickstart diet, these are such a treat, and are again super quick to make. The ketogenic diet that appeared on the TV show is a type of low-carb, high-fat diet, which I love and truly believe in. Originally ketogenic diets were developed to control epilepsy, then they became popular with the body-building crowd to reduce body fat. These macaroons freeze perfectly, too, so stash them in twos.

ZERO-CARB KETO COCONUT MACAROONS

100g unsweetened desiccated coconut
2 tbsp Sukrin (a sugar substitute that contains no carbs and is available from most supermarkets and healthfood shops)
1 tbsp vanilla extract
1 tbsp coconut oil
2–3 egg whites
pinch of salt

Preheat the oven to 190°C/gas mark 5 and line a baking tray with baking paper.

Whisk the egg whites with a balloon whisk or a freestanding electric mixer until stiff, then gently fold in the rest of the ingredients – SO EASY.

Use a small ice-cream scoop or a tablespoon to scoop 8 portions onto the prepared baking tray. Bake in the oven for 12 minutes until golden.

Remove from the oven and allow to cool a little so that they firm up. Eat warm or leave to cool completely and store in an airtight container for up to 3 days.

FAT (g): 0.5
PROTEIN (g): 1.5
CARBS (g): 29.9
FIBRE (g): 1.7
CALORIES: 133
SERVES: 1

Always try to keep some chopped bananas in the freezer for this quick, satisfying, cheap and versatile dessert. It can be whipped up in under a minute, so it's perfect for those instant cravings. I enjoy a serving of this several times a week.

INSTANT BANANA ICE CREAM, 3 WAYS

1 large banana, chopped and frozen until hard
1 tsp honey
1 tsp vanilla extract
2 tbsp almond milk

Blend the banana, honey and vanilla in a food processor just until smooth. Don't overdo it, as it can quickly liquify. While the machine is still running, trickle in the milk (you might not need it all), occasionally scraping down the sides and continue to blend until smooth. Enjoy immediately as a 'soft serve' ice cream or pop back in the freezer for about 10 minutes to firm up.

Try adding any of these to the blender at the same time as the bananas:
½ scoop of protein powder
50g frozen blueberries, raspberries or strawberries
5g cocoa powder and 10g chopped hazelnuts
1 tsp ground cinnamon and 2 chopped juicy dates like medjool

FAT (g): 5.8
PROTEIN (g): 4.8
CARBS (g): 8.6
FIBRE (g): 1.3
CALORIES: 109
MAKES: 12

These balls are a protein-packed sweet treat you can enjoy either before a gym session or to help you repair afterwards. Skip the processed protein bars and make your own. I always have a little bag of these in my gym bag.

PRE- OR POST- GYM ENERGY BALLS

125g peanut butter or almond butter
1 tbsp raw cacao or cocoa powder
2 tbsp unsweetened desiccated coconut,
    lightly toasted
1 tsp black or white sesame seeds, lightly toasted
60ml honey or maple syrup
finely grated zest of 1 orange (optional)
1 tbsp protein powder (vanilla or chocolate)
pinch of salt
1 tsp vanilla extract
20g oats

Blend all the ingredients together in a mini food processor until smooth and the mixture clumps into a ball. Portion the mixture into 12 pieces and roll into balls. They are ready to eat straightaway. Keep them in an airtight container for several days.

FAT (g): 9.4
PROTEIN (g): 2.2
CARBS (g): 5.8
FIBRE (g): 1.6
CALORIES: 119
MAKES: 10

My twist on the popular, commercially made peanut-butter cup – this will save you nearly 4g sugar per cup.

ALMOND BUTTER CUPS

100g good-quality dark chocolate (at least 70% cocoa solids), roughly chopped
1 tsp vanilla extract
2 tbsp coconut oil
2 tbsp honey
10 tsp natural almond butter
few pinches of sea salt

Get 10 mini cupcake cases ready.

Melt the chocolate, vanilla, coconut oil and honey in a heatproof bowl set over a pan of gently simmering water. When melted, pour half of the mixture into the bottom of the cupcake cases. At this stage you can freeze them for 10 minutes to set the bottom layer, if you like, but it's not essential.

Add 1 tsp almond butter to each case and top with the remaining melted chocolate mix. Top each almond butter cup with a pinch of sea salt and chill in the fridge or freeze until set, about 15 minutes. Enjoy one – or two MAX if your calories allow.

INDEX

Publishing director: Sarah Lavelle
Creative director: Helen Lewis
Editor: Céline Hughes
Design concept: Smith & Gilmour
Designer: Katherine Keeble
Photography: Louise Hagger and John Davis
Food stylist: Georgina Davies
Props stylist: Tonia Shuttleworth
Consultant Dietitian: Sian Porter
Production: Stephen Lang, Vincent Smith

First published in 2017 by Quadrille Publishing
Pentagon House, 52–54 Southwark Street,
London SE1 1UN

Quadrille Publishing is an
imprint of Hardie Grant
hardiegrant.com
quadrille.com

Cataloguing in Publication Data: a catalogue record
for this book is available from the British Library.

978 1 78713 159 0

Printed in Germany

ACKNOWLEDGEMENTS

THANK YOU:
Mam, for absolutely everything from Day One. I hope
I make you proud.

My agent Katherine Stonehouse, for believing in me all
those years ago, and for your patience.

Ryan, my soulmate, for your support in writing this
book, for all the laughs and the love and all the extra
hours in the shop doing what needed to be done so I
could achieve my dream.

Sarah, Céline, Katherine, Sian and the team
at Quadrille for seeing my vision and doing an
ABSOLUTELY sterling job of bringing it to life –
thank you.

The team at Little Gem: Kurt for giving me a chance
and taking a punt – I'll never forget it; and Ben and
Natasha for making such an amazing show and for
allowing me to be a part of it, year after year.

Ryan, Kristian, Kirbey and Jac, my best mates in the
world, for the laughs and support and countless pep
talks when I doubt myself.

Joshua Leonard for the hair styling through the book –
my little Aussie superstar.